No ethical issue keeps me up at night as does the question of artificial intelligence. The reason for my dismay is that the church doesn't seem to be thinking very deeply about these matters at all, even as we move into a technological revolution that could prove to be Gutenberg-level in its implications. This book is a balm for anxiety in the age of technological disruption. No evangelical has thought and written more clearly on these matters than Jason Thacker. In this monumental work, he avoids both naivete and paranoia about AI. The years ahead will require wise Christians in a time of smart robots. This book shows the way.

> *Russell Moore,* president, Ethics and
> Religious Liberty Commission

Harnessing technology in our world, especially in education and medicine, can help us live productive and fulfilling lives. Yet Thacker reminds us that we must learn to do so in ways that glorify God and protect the innocent among us. Great read for parents!

> *Jeb Bush,* former governor of Florida

As more aspects of our economy and of our daily lives are automated, we have an increasing burden to question our new technologies. Jason Thacker's *The Age of AI* is an excellent introduction for those seeking to understand both these coming changes and the truths about humanity that will not change. This book offers a foundation for future reflection on life in a world inseparable from artificial intelligence, as well as practical tools for navigating your family and community through these choppy waters.

> *Ben Sasse,* US senator, Nebraska; author, *Them:*
> *Why We Hate Each Other—and How to Heal*

There are some things you don't know you need until it's too late. What Jason Thacker has done in this work is prepare us for a future where we will need to think clearly and biblically about artificial intelligence. *The Age of AI* is a book for our time as the use of AI is rapidly advancing. It is deeply researched but accessible to the average reader, theologically rich, and filled with wise counsel. I'm grateful for this book.

> *Trillia Newbell,* author, *Sacred Endurance,*
> *If God Is for Us,* and *Fear and Faith*

Technology rightly applied can be powerful for humanity and the church. AI is challenging us to consider carefully how it can be shaped for God's kingdom and to understand its risks. Jason puts all of this into historical and scriptural context for each of us to deepen our insights into this critical topic.

> *Pat Gelsinger,* CEO VMware; founder, Transforming
> the Bay with Christ; author, *The Juggling Act*

AI is an important subject, not just for computer scientists but for everyone, with implications for areas ranging from work and family life to medicine and commerce. Finding a thoughtful Christian voice on this topic is rare, and so this timely book is a welcome contribution to the ongoing conversation about the responsible use of AI.

> *Derek C. Schuurman,* professor of computer
> science, Calvin University

Rapid advances in technology present Christians in the twenty-first century with profound ethical and stewardship questions we dare not ignore. In this book, Jason Thacker brings an authentic Christian intelligence to the vexing and high-velocity quandaries of artificial intelligence. You need to read this book, intelligently.

> *R. Albert Mohler Jr.,* president, The Southern
> Baptist Theological Seminary

I recommend *The Age of AI* highly and without reservation. In it, Jason Thacker employs a theological framework—drawing upon the *imago Dei* and the Great Commandment especially—within which he addresses pressing questions about artificial intelligence as it relates to individuals and families, as well as to the medical, military, and data industries. Thacker's style is approachable and thus will prove helpful for a broad audience of thoughtful Christians.

> *Bruce Riley Ashford,* author, *The Gospel of Our
> King*; provost and professor of theology and culture,
> Southeastern Baptist Theological Seminary

The age of AI is not a *Jetsons* fantasy of the distant future. It's here. And this new age raises challenging theological questions. Jason Thacker helps us prepare for this imminent future in *The Age of AI*. It's a practical and valuable early entry in what will surely be a growing body of Christian writing and thinking on AI in coming years.

> **Brett McCracken,** senior editor, The Gospel
> Coalition; author, *Uncomfortable: The Awkward*
> *and Essential Challenge of Christian Community*

The Age of AI informs us and assists us in envisioning a future that is filled with tools, influences, opportunities, and challenges relating to artificial intelligence. While many may fear the unknown future before us, Jason Thacker presents the imperative need to always lift up the constancy of the image of God and the dignity of all human life as presented in the Holy Scriptures, the Bible. I am thankful Jason's book can help churches, pastors, theologians, and Christian leaders in all vocations to wrestle through this current topic, always being committed to what this book states profoundly: God-given dignity isn't ours to assign or remove.

> **Dr. Ronnie Floyd,** president and CEO, Southern
> Baptist Convention Executive Committee

Our culture is worried about issues surrounding AI but often lacks insight into how to think wisely about this technology. This is because modern culture is disconnected from some underlying and necessary presuppositions: God is real, we are made in his image, and we cannot create as he creates. Jason Thacker offers keen insight into AI, how to think about it, and how to relate to it in a way that is focused on these truths.

> **Erick Erickson,** editor, *The Resurgent*

As a Christian parent and pastor trying to live my life faithfully engaged with the surrounding culture while also leading others, I already feel behind when it comes to many discussions concerning technology and our changing world. I am thankful for someone like Jason Thacker who is skilled in articulating the state of our digital world and who also is well informed on the future realities and implications headed our way, especially in the realm of AI. We need

Christians who can inform the church with a biblical worldview how to navigate through this digital age that is only going to increase in the days ahead. Not only is Jason informed, he's at the center of the conversation, exactly where we need Christians to find themselves. While the digital world changes daily, God's Word never falls behind. I am grateful Jason Thacker is writing with an everlasting truth in this ever-changing culture.

> *Dean Inserra,* lead pastor, City Church, Tallahassee, Florida; author, *The Unsaved Christian: Reaching Cultural Christianity with the Gospel*

For far too long, evangelicals have found ourselves trailing behind the culture and desperate to keep up. From our current vantage point, we can see that artificial intelligence and emerging technologies will soon confront Christians with various questions we've never had to grapple with before. In *The Age of AI*, Jason Thacker serves as a helpful guide for believers and the church to understand and prepare for the challenges of the future.

> *J. D. Greear,* pastor, The Summit Church; president, Southern Baptist Convention

THE AGE OF AI

ARTIFICIAL INTELLIGENCE AND THE FUTURE OF HUMANITY

JASON THACKER

To my wife and boys:
without you none of this would be possible
and with you I know we can face
anything as we follow Christ

CONTENTS

FOREWORD

When I was doing my doctoral studies in philosophy, I participated in a seminar in which we talked a lot about minds and machines. We dealt with questions about whether computers could ever really think in the way humans do, and whether they could replicate our form of consciousness.

We considered a lot of examples, but they were mainly hypothetical. A favorite was the Turing test—Jason Thacker has a nice discussion of it in this book—where we had to speculate about what it would take for a computer to fool us into thinking that we were communicating with another person.

Again, these were all pretty much hypothetical cases. At the time—this was in the late 1960s—we had few examples to go on, so we did a lot of speculation. There were, of course, some chess-playing computers at the time, but there was quite a bit of skepticism about whether they were really playing the game, as opposed to simply going through possible moves that they had been programmed to process.

These days we are dealing with more than hypotheticals. I frequently ask Siri to send my wife a text about when I will arrive home from a meeting, and when Siri tells me that the text has been sent, I sometimes find myself saying, "Thank you!" That may not be a successful outcome of a Turing test, but I do wonder on occasion about the philosophical and theological implications of my impulsive response.

In this marvelous book, Jason Thacker gives us much help in thinking through those implications. For Christians, the questions get at the heart of things. Discussions of artificial intelligence typically focus on the degree to which new technological devices are starting to be like us. Will they replace us in some significant way? Will they even surpass us in their ability to accomplish things that we always thought were unique to human efforts?

Jason Thacker is aware of the profound character of these concerns for Christians. The Bible begins with a clear portrayal of the "us"—human beings, male and female, created in the very image and likeness of the living God. But we learn also that our first parents soon decided to be their own gods, thus getting all of us into a horrible mess. Our sinful condition means that we have a difficult time finding the rightful place of the "us" in the overall scheme of things. Sometimes we define humanity down, reducing ourselves to the level of animals. And sometimes we define ourselves up, as in the recent transhumanist patterns of thought that are nicely explained in these pages.

What we Christians cannot settle for is a simple rejection of technological advances. The Lord can use artificial intelligence for good things, which means that we must think seriously—grounded in fidelity to the Scriptures—about important theological questions. This book is an excellent guide for doing just that. And as Jason Thacker makes abundantly clear, the issues are not abstract concerns. He provides splendid insights into what they mean for raising our children, faithful engagement in our daily work, communicating the gospel, and much more. I am deeply grateful for what I have learned in reading this book about matters that are of crucial importance for the life of the Christian community.

—*Richard J. Mouw*

CHAPTER 1

FOUNDATION

Man and Machine

When I mention artificial intelligence, the first thing that comes to people's minds is likely to be science fiction stories, such as the movie *I, Robot*. You know, robots plotting to enslave humanity. Or perhaps a humanoid robot learning to demonstrate and feel human emotions and eager to integrate into the human world, as Andrew did in *Bicentennial Man*. Artificial intelligence seems far off and futuristic to us. As a result, we haven't given much thought to it and aren't sure that we will need to anytime soon.

For all of the sci-fi movies and TV shows that flood our screens year after year, we might have missed that we have already welcomed various forms of artificial intelligence into our families and homes. Artificial intelligence (AI) is a crucial piece of many forms of technology today, including smart phones, social media, search platforms, and smart-home devices. Famed computer scientist and futurist Ray Kurzweil says that "if all of the AI systems decided to go on strike tomorrow, our civilization would be crippled: We couldn't get money from our bank, and indeed, our money would disappear; communication, transportation, and manufacturing would all grind to a halt."[1] AI is everywhere, even if you don't recognize it. But for all of its advantages and benefits, AI is also challenging some of the basic principles of life, causing many to wonder about human nature and what really makes us distinct from the rest of creation. AI is doing things like driving cars around our streets and automating countless jobs that were created for humans. AI is changing everything about our world and society. And we aren't prepared.

Artificial intelligence is the technology of today and tomorrow. So where do we begin our journey to understand it? We must begin where everything began: in the pages of Scripture. Scripture is our guide to navigating this world with wisdom and ultimately points us to Jesus Christ, the founder and perfecter of our faith (Heb. 12:2).

SEEKING WISDOM

Scripture never mentions anything about artificial intelligence. That likely isn't a surprise to you. Many of the issues we face in life are not explicitly addressed in the Bible, but God's Word supplies wisdom to us as we encounter tough questions.

So I propose two questions to aid us in our journey to apply God's Word to artificial intelligence:

1. What does it mean to be human?
2. What is technology and artificial intelligence?

WHAT DOES IT MEAN TO BE HUMAN?

The book of Genesis describes how God created everything in our world. He created the heavens and the earth. He created everything that has ever been known. Before the creation of space and time, only God existed, in the eternal Trinity as Father, Son, and Holy Spirit (Col. 1:13–17).

Not only did God create the heavens and the earth but he created everything on our planet. He created the waters of the sea and the grass of the land. He created the birds of the air and the teeming life of the seemingly bottomless oceans.

Not only did God choose to create the heavens and the earth, the waters and the land, the birds of the air and the fish of the sea but he chose to create humanity, and he did so for a purpose.

The Image of God

Humanity is distinct from everything in God's creation. There is something unique about us compared with everything else that God made. Genesis 1:26 says, "Let us make man in our image, after our likeness." God chose to make us in his image. He crafted us to be like him. After God created man, he said that he was "very good," as opposed to just "good" like he had said on the previous five days. But what was so unique about humanity?

God gave us specific jobs and responsibilities to perform as we seek to reflect him in this world. "And God blessed them. And God said to them, 'Be fruitful and multiply and fill the earth and subdue it, and have dominion over the fish of the sea and over the birds of the heavens and over every living thing that moves on the earth'" (1:28). Our job is to be fruitful and multiply, to fill the earth and subdue it, and to take dominion over all of creation. This means raising families, working the ground, and caring for creation.

To "work the ground" is another way of saying to do our jobs by using the abilities God has given us. That means being the best plumber, designer, student, leader, or parent that you can be to the glory of God. God has given each of his image-bearers gifts to use as they seek the good of society. These jobs are not a result of sin or a punishment for our rebellion. They were given to us so that we might reflect him in the world.

God gave us minds and bodies to do the jobs he created us to do. Our minds and bodies allow us to reflect God as we work. For example, we can be creative and design things unlike anything else in creation. As part of our creativity, we make technology to aid us in our God-given responsibilities. Genesis 2:15 tells us that "God took the man and put him in the garden of Eden to work it and keep it." What God calls us to do, he provides for us to do. He gives us the tools to fulfill our callings.

One gift that God has given us is our minds. Having minds means that we are able to use reason to process, plan, and execute what God has given us the responsibility to do. With our minds, we are able to design and create in ways that nothing else in creation is able to do.

Even the smartest of animals—such as the beaver, which constructs a massive structure made of precisely laid sticks, or the lesser known cathedral termite, which builds homes fifteen feet tall that function as self-sustaining megacities—cannot compare with the abilities of humans. We are able to use our minds to create technology and even forms of artificial intelligence that can mimic how we, as humans, think and plan. There is no other part of creation that has been given the minds and talents that God has bestowed on us as his image-bearers.

As you and I reflect God with our creative abilities, we are able to make things that allow us to live our callings as workers in easier and more efficient ways that benefit all of society. Think about all of the tools that we use each day that make our lives easier. From hammers and nails to digital devices like smart phones and computers, we design and create tools that allow us to work in a broken world that is not the way God designed it to be.

The Rebellion

Genesis 3 describes when things fell apart. Adam and Eve were tempted to believe a lie about God and they decided to rebel against him. Their rebellion is our rebellion (1 Cor. 15:22). This rebellion brought sin into the world and broke the natural order of things. Our lives and work are more difficult than they were designed to be. Things don't work as they should. Sin brought sickness, death, brokenness, and shame into our world.

But for all of the effects of sin in our lives and our world, the image of God in us was not lost. We are still able to create, design, and make things, but it is a much harder process in our fallen world. Work comes with pitfalls, unintended consequences, technological failures, and things that don't operate the way they are designed to. Also, the purpose behind technology is skewed in our minds. We misuse and abuse the gifts that God has given us and contort them for sinful and prideful means. We use technology to hurt others, to distract and distance ourselves from God, and to make ourselves feel more important than we are.

Given how we were created and the work that we are called to do, what is the proper purpose and use of technology amid this brokenness?

WHAT IS TECHNOLOGY?

Technology is a tool that helps us live out our God-given callings. This is one of the most important things for us to learn as we engage the topic of technology and artificial intelligence. Because we often see the tremendous power that technology has over our lives, we are tempted to treat technology as more than a tool, as something with a value similar to our own if it is powerful enough or does enough work on its own. Technology will be misused and abused by broken people just like you and me.

Nowhere in Scripture is a tool or a technology condemned for being evil. Scripture shows that technology and tools can be used for both good and evil. Even if a tool was designed for evil, the tool itself isn't evil. What is sinful isn't the sword but how people choose to use it. It can be used for righteous purposes like standing up for justice against those who are evil, but it can also be used to hurt or kill the innocent. While the technology isn't moral in that sense, it does carry with it the effects of sin and brokenness. Technology is not morally neutral, because it influences and changes us each time we use it.

Technology expands what is possible for humans to do. It can be best thought of as a catalyst or an accelerant for change because it opens new opportunities for humans to live in this world. Broken, sinful, and evil humans are the ones given the abilities to create these tools and the ones who can choose how we use them. Paul reminds us that each of us has fallen short and needs to repent (Rom. 3:23). The world itself did not sin. Our tools did not rebel. We did.

The story of Cain and Abel is a great example of this truth about the purpose and use of technology. Both Cain and Abel were created by God with specific skills and talents. Both used tools (early forms of technology) to work the ground and care for animals. But Cain sinned and chose to use his God-given strength and abilities to kill a fellow image-bearer. He chose to take the good gifts that God gave him and use them for evil and selfish purposes.

TECHNOLOGY IS NOT NEW

In our digital world, it is easy for us to believe that technology always takes the form of digital and computer technology, limiting our idea of technology to our smart phones and computers. But even crude tools used to cultivate the ground and construct things are forms of technology. Shovels, hoes, hammers, nails, and saws are all technological innovations. These tools were revolutionary pieces of technology. They changed everything about our lives, from the foods we ate to the places we lived.

One of the most important pieces of technology in all of human history is the printing press. Johannes Gutenberg is credited with inventing the world's first movable-type printing press in 1450, and it revolutionized the world. It allowed books and other materials to be mass produced cheaply and efficiently, and made them available for mass distribution, not just for the wealthy or those with high status in society.

The printing press is the main reason that you have this book in your hands and even have your own copy of the

Bible. Before the printing press, each Bible was hand copied by scribes. Not only were these Bibles prohibitively expensive because of how much time they took to create but they also could contain errors because they were being copied by hand. The printing press helped to mitigate these copying errors as well as to bring the cost of books down so that common people could directly engage with the ideas in them. This technological advancement changed society not only at that time but for all generations to come by giving people access to more information than was ever thought possible.

But even as the printing press was a catalyst for good, it also expanded the possibilities for evil in our world. Without the printing press, we likely would not have twenty-four-hour cable news networks and the rise of fake news.[2] This is because the printing press began the process of spreading news and information throughout communities which previously didn't enjoy these freedoms. With all of this information and freedom, people were able to connect in ways that were unthinkable prior to the printing press. All of this eventually gave rise to the press and mass media that we enjoy today as a natural extension of the free flow of information and exchange of ideas. While access to information is a good thing for democracy and society, it also can be misused to promote sinful and evil things. The printing press also led to the distribution of pornography by sinful human beings because it facilitated copying text and later images for distribution to a wider society. From these two examples, we can see how technology itself isn't evil but can be used by broken and sinful people for evil purposes. Technology is amoral in that sense, but it is a catalyst for change and an opportunity for both good and evil.

We are at another turning point in human technological development. Artificial intelligence is, even now, revolutionizing nearly every area of our society, including our lives, our families, and our jobs. It is able to perform tasks for us with or without our involvement, unlike prior technological developments like the printing press that were driven manually by a human operator. Artificial intelligence is now performing many of the tasks that our culture was built on and is disrupting our society in ways that we cannot even fathom. From processing massive amounts of data with ease to replacing millions of people's jobs, AI is changing everything.

Technology is a catalyst for change and an opportunity for both good and evil.

WHAT IS ARTIFICIAL INTELLIGENCE?

My family has a digital assistant working in our home that is incredibly smart, never takes a break, and never complains about its job. A couple of years ago, we purchased a Google Home Mini to integrate with other smart household devices, and we've found fun ways to use it, especially with our toddler. My oldest son was learning different animal sounds, and we asked the assistant to make a number of animal sounds for him. But it couldn't find one of the requested sounds, and its response struck me: "I can't help you with that right now. But I am always learning." Learning vast amounts of information used to be something only humans could do, but today we have many machines and AI-empowered systems that do just that.

Artificial intelligence is an emerging field of technology defined as nonbiological intelligence, where a machine is programmed to accomplish complex goals by applying knowledge to the task at hand. Because it's nonbiological, AI can be copied and reprogrammed at relatively low cost. In certain forms, it is extremely flexible and can be harnessed for great good or for ill.

Google Home is a popular example, but there are far more advanced AI systems than this being used in a variety of applications such as business, medicine, and finance. In 2017, a set of videos of walking robots from Google and Boston Dynamics went viral on the internet. These AI-based systems did things that astonished most viewers (and even many in the AI community) with their ability to walk and even traverse rough terrain with ease.[3]

AI systems have become so advanced so quickly that many wonder what these systems will accomplish in the future as they become smarter and human intervention becomes less necessary. This is not a sci-fi fantasy. It's reality.

NOT JUST FUN AND GAMES

The term artificial intelligence was coined in 1956 by John McCarthy, a scientist who is considered one of the fathers of AI. That year, he organized the Dartmouth Summer Research Project on Artificial Intelligence, which was a gathering of experts who brainstormed about the possibility of AI.

McCarthy's proposal for the research project read in part:

> We propose that a two-month, ten-man study of artificial intelligence be carried out during the summer of 1956 at Dartmouth College in Hanover, New Hampshire. The study is to proceed on the basis of the conjecture that every aspect of learning or any other feature of

intelligence can in principle be so precisely described that a machine can be made to simulate it. An attempt will be made to find how to make machines use language, form abstractions and concepts, solve kinds of problems now reserved for humans, and improve themselves. We think that a significant advance can be made in one or more of these problems if a carefully selected group of scientists work on it together for a summer.[4]

The intent of artificial intelligence was to make machines that could, like humans, use language, form concepts, solve difficult problems, and improve themselves through learning. McCarthy and his team proposed designing AI systems to play board games, because of their complexity, rules-based play, and the relatively innocuous effects of winning or losing. The stakes were low regardless of how the systems performed. Between the 1960s and the 1990s, there were exciting breakthroughs, rapid development, unbridled expectations, and then ultimately disappointments. Often the initial breakthroughs slowed because of the lack of computer power and the limited ability of developers to design machines to think or perform highly complex tasks.

In 2016, Google's London-based DeepMind division created an AI system called AlphaGo that dethroned the reigning Go champion. Go is an ancient abstract strategy board game played on a nineteen-by-nineteen-inch board with black and white stones. Created more than 2,500 years ago in China, Go is extremely complex even though it has simple rules. It is believed that there are at least 2×10^{170} possible moves on the game board, and this means most players are forced to use their intuition rather than memory to win the game.

The AlphaGo team used a type of AI learning called a deep neural network. Neural networks were introduced more than two decades ago and have grown in complexity ever since. The AlphaGo team built on years of research into layering neural networks, which allowed AlphaGo to function more like a human brain, to mimic how we think and process information. While at its core AlphaGo still processed data like prior AI systems, it was not programmed with a set of good moves and strategies. It was able to learn from watching thousands of Go games and applied what it learned to a given match. It became better with each match. When AlphaGo beat the Go world champion, Lee Sedol, four to one in a five-game match, the victory brought a new level of popular predictions and excitement about the future of AI. But only time will tell how this victory will change the field of AI and its impact on our lives.

THE WORLDVIEW BEHIND AI

As I've written in this chapter, technology is amoral but acts as a catalyst that expands the opportunities for humanity to pursue. It is not good or evil in itself but can be designed and used for good and evil purposes. We are able to use technology for the glory of God and the betterment of society, or we can use it to push aside the dignity of others created in God's image for sinful and contorted means.

AI is already being used to demean certain people and deny them fundamental human rights. Countries like China, Russia, North Korea, and Egypt have deployed AI facial recognition systems to control political dissidents. But this same technology can also be used ethically to identify criminals, stop terrorist threats, and even allow you to pay for a meal at a KFC in China just by smiling at a camera.[5]

Though the purpose behind the creation of a given technology can be morally complicated or even evil, that doesn't mean that God is unable to redeem it for a noble and righteous use. To use tools properly, though, we must understand the worldviews behind them and the motivations that drive their creation. As we engage these understandings of the world, remember that God calls us to "see to it that no one takes you captive by philosophy and empty deceit, according to human tradition, according to the elemental spirits of the world, and not according to Christ" (Col. 2:8).

Many see artificial intelligence through a materialist worldview, which simply states that everything in our universe, even our thoughts and minds, is reducible to matter and that nothing spiritual or supernatural exists. Everything about you and your life is reducible to some chemical and natural reaction. Materialists rely heavily on the theory of evolution from Charles Darwin's 1859 book, *On the Origin of Species*, which offers an explanation for how humanity came to be and how our world developed over time. While not all of those who hold to evolution are materialists, all materialists believe in some form of evolution and deny the existence of any creator God or special creation. Some see AI as the next stage of our world's evolution. It is argued that human beings are nothing more than a set of organic algorithms or a biological computer, albeit an extremely complex one. We have arrived at this stage of history as the most advanced life form over millions of years of natural selection, but there is nothing inherently unique about us other than the fact that we survived the test of time.

From this perspective, humans are just more complex than the rest of the world, including the animal kingdom. Even though certain species might be more powerful or better than humans in one or two aspects, we are the total package of brains and brawn. We are able to do things that nothing else in the world can dream of doing. But that doesn't mean that it will always be that way. As AI becomes exponentially more complex and adept at problem solving, acquires language and processing skills, and begins to think on its own, we will take a back seat to this higher form of life.

Materialists often argue that AI will eventually take over every area of society. It will replace us in the workforce and even in our homes. We won't be needed because our value is tied to what we do rather than who we are. We will be outdated because something new and better will come along. Max Tegmark, an MIT physics professor and cofounder of the Future of Life Institute, argues that AI is going to be the next stage of evolution and will at some point take over as the most advanced lifeform in the world. He explains in his book *Life 3.0: Being Human in the Age of Artificial Intelligence* that the next stage in evolution will be superadvanced AI systems that aren't bound by the limits of biology like human beings are. This new form of life will be able to upgrade its software (learning) and its hardware (physical structure).[6] Yuval Noah Harari describes a similar idea when he claims that humanity is simply a set of organic algorithms that will one day be matched in complexity and then soon outperformed by these superadvanced digital algorithms.[7]

These new algorithms are often described as artificial general intelligence (AGI) leading to superintelligence. But as we'll see in chapter 8, the timeline for and even the possibility of such advanced forms of AI have been more the stuff of sci-fi movies than reality. There's significant disagreement among AI experts regarding whether such developments are possible and when, if ever, they could happen. No one knows at this point.

OUR NEW GOLDEN CALF

You might be tempted to think that artificial intelligence is of interest only to computer geeks, sci-fi novelists, and researchers. But as the story of my Google Home device illustrates, artificial intelligence is no longer just a tool for geeks and programmers. It is being implemented in nearly every area of our society, and it is quickly becoming the framework that allows us to function as we do each day.

Take Netflix and Amazon, for example. Both companies use highly advanced algorithms and AI systems to recommend movies and products to keep us engaged with their platforms. These systems make decisions based on a trove of data collected on us and thousands of people around us to help determine what we might like to see or purchase next. This is also true on social media platforms that display messages that they think we will like and engage with to keep us coming back for more. But AI isn't limited to just commercial products that make our lives easier. It is driving many areas that are invisible to most of us, including weapons systems used by our government and even our financial markets. AI undergirds so much automation today because it is able to process massive amounts of data, drawing connections that humans might miss or are unable to see, and usually doing so faster and with greater precision than humans can in these narrow tasks.

AI is producing results and accomplishing goals that amaze even the most well informed in the AI community. This leads many to rightfully question how we will engage with these machines and what our relationship with them will be like.

We are on the cusp of something new, but we must see behind the glitz and glam that AI produces. Are we creating yet another tool, or have we fooled ourselves into thinking that we are creating something greater than us? While the benefits of AI are many, the threat to human dignity is real and must be addressed by thoughtful Christians.

In Exodus 32, we read that Moses ascended Mt. Sinai to speak with God. God had rescued his people from the Egyptians and provided for them as they journeyed away from Egypt. Even so, unrest grew among the people while Moses was on the mountain. They told Aaron to make from their gold and jewelry a god before which they could bow down and worship. They fell victim to the age-old notion that because we can't see something with our eyes, it doesn't exist. They doubted that God existed and that he cared for them. They created something that they believed would be worthy to rule over them, protect them, and provide for them. This golden calf was an idol, a fake god. It had no power other than the power that the people gave it.

While the benefits of AI are many, the threat to human dignity is real and must be addressed by thoughtful Christians.

They did not know what they were making. They did not understand their rebellion and that the golden calf was a weak substitute for the life-giving presence of God. They fooled themselves into thinking that they were making something greater than themselves.

The same may be true with artificial intelligence. Many believe that we are ushering in a new world order where these machines will save us from ourselves and protect us in ways that we never thought of before.

As with every new development, Christians must proclaim who Scripture reveals God to be, and who we are as created in his image. The tools we make are to be used well and not used to rule over us. We need to apply God's Word so that we might magnify him and care for our neighbors (Matt. 22:37–39).

You likely have already been thinking about how tools like your smart assistant are changing you, or have questioned how this new technology will affect your family. You might wonder what the future holds if the predictions of massive job losses to AI and automation come true. You might even fear a future of killer robots bent on destroying humanity. As we are faced with challenges to our faith and livelihoods, we must start with a foundational understanding of who we are and how technology affects our communities.

We must engage these issues, rather than respond after their effects are widely felt. But we don't have to face today or tomorrow with fear. God is sovereign and his Word is sufficient for every good work, so we are able to walk with confidence as we apply his Word to these challenges with wisdom and guided by his Spirit.

The question is not if AI will affect us and our churches but when. Are you ready? How are we to think about AI? How must we engage with this debate over these fundamental ideas? The answers are more complicated than you might think.

In this book, we will look at several areas that are being revolutionized by artificial intelligence, and we will seek to apply God's wisdom to them. We will discover some of the great benefits AI will provide us in the future, but we will also see some of its dangers. We will explore how AI is changing us as individuals, as families, and as a society. We will then see AI's disruptive impact on our economy. Next, we will look at how AI is changing war and even our notions of privacy and security. We will conclude by examining what the future of AI might hold, how we are responsible for that future, and how we can move forward honoring God and loving our neighbors as ourselves. Let's explore together how to navigate the age of AI.

CHAPTER 2

SELF

Alexa, Are You There?

I magine you are sitting on your couch after a long day. You pull out your phone to see Twitter updates from your friends and to check on the news. You keep scrolling through your feed full of funny cat videos, updates on your favorite sports team, and posts from your friends. You scroll past the perfect dinner that your friend cooked and framed just right so that their followers would be jealous of their latest creation. You are just hoping that you have a box of mac and cheese for dinner tonight.

You notice that you have a new message. As you click on it, you see it is from an old high school friend who just joined Twitter but still has the infamous egg profile picture. You normally don't respond to messages from people online, but this is an old friend. You don't give much thought to it and then go back to your updates. Soon your friend follows up asking about some of your friends from high school, and something seems a little bit off with the interaction. But you are probably reading into things, right? You chalk it up to bad memory and put your phone on the charger as you head off to bed.

THE TURING TEST

In 1950, Alan Turing proposed one of the most provocative tests that the world had ever seen. Turing was an English mathematician, a computer scientist, and a pioneer in the field of artificial intelligence. During World War II, Turing served the Allied cause by helping to break the infamous Enigma code that Nazi Germany used to encrypt radio communications throughout the war. Historians believe that Turing's breaking of the Nazi code helped to end the war many years early. Turing was a brilliant man whose life was cut short at the young age of forty-one. One of his many contributions to society is the Turing test, which is designed to test whether a machine could be said to be intelligent.

The test was designed to determine whether a computer can fool a human into thinking that they are talking with a fellow human being. According to Turing, if a machine passed the test, it would be shown to be intelligent. The test involves a human evaluator who is told that they will communicate with two people only through the use of text on a computer screen. They are informed that one person is a real human being and the other is a computer. Based on the text-only conversation, the evaluator is to decide which is the computer and which is the real person. If the machine successfully fools the evaluator, it passes the test because it successfully passed itself off as a human being.

While this test has been used for decades in the field of

artificial intelligence to determine if a computer can exhibit intelligent behavior, the debate still rages to this day because of varying definitions of intelligence and what makes humanity distinct from the rest of creation.

So did you have an encounter with a high school classmate on Twitter that night or were you fooled by a computer bot that gathered data as it tricked you into thinking it was a real person? Lest you think that this example is a bit too creepy, extreme, or futuristic, you may soon be subject to a Turing-like test the next time you answer your phone. Spoiler alert: the computer wins.

WELCOME TO THE FUTURE

In May 2018, Google announced a groundbreaking technology that it hoped would revolutionize the way humans interact with computers. Google Duplex is an AI system that can make phone calls for you as your personal assistant. During the debut presentation, Duplex called to book a woman's salon appointment and to make a restaurant reservation for four without any human intervention on the user's side. After the call, it sent a push notification to let the user know that it had completed its task.

Remarkably, Duplex sounded almost identical to a human being and fooled the employees on the other end of the calls, who had no idea they were communicating with a computer. This AI system uses a technique called natural language processing and incorporates various umms, ahhs, as well as pauses to sound more natural. You also can even change the voice of Duplex to suit your preference, just as you can on Apple's Siri or the old Garmin GPS units.

The system employs machine learning to process what is being said, interact with the other caller in real time, pace itself, account for variables or misunderstandings, and speak in a natural way that is virtually indistinguishable from a human in the context of a phone call. The system was able to learn these methods of communication from a set of recorded calls given to it by the developers. It processed these test calls, learned from them, then made practice phone calls with human supervision. The system was able to learn from its mistakes and gain new knowledge through repetition. Soon after these test calls, it no longer needed human supervision and was able to function on its own with a high level of precision in very specific applications.

The debut of this groundbreaking advance in AI received mixed reviews. Many reporters and observers were excited by its potential, and the technology made front page news in tech publications and on blogs. But there were also some skeptical reviews about how Google could protect the user's privacy and how the AI was essentially fooling people by not identifying itself as a machine. My first reaction to the announcement was excitement about how AI is advancing and how it will help so many people. This use of AI could save me so much time in the future by automating some of the mundane tasks that I tend to forget, like booking a haircut, and I could see the system stepping in for me during those crazy-long waits on the phone when I am trying to fix some issue or pay a bill. But I also was concerned about what impact the technology would have on how we see each other as human beings. Should it be used on an unknowing clerk or employee at your favorite restaurant? Could it be used to impersonate your voice in the future similar to how deepfakes can make it look like you said and did things that never happened? How might it be used to take advantage of our neighbors rather than empower them? Does it blur the line between human and machine too much?

In reaction to the outcry of reporters and the tech community, Google clarified that the AI system will identify itself as the Google assistant and inform the person on the other end of the line that they are indeed talking with a computer. But regardless of how this technology might be used, it is easy to see that advances like this are not confined to the computer labs and big technology companies. They affect our daily lives as we increasingly incorporate technology into every area of life.

Because of how sophisticated AI has become, many of us are beginning to question the nature of intelligence and what it means to be human. Many hope that language processing will enable us one day to interact with robots the same way we do with other human beings. But the danger is that we might dumb down what it means to be human, assigning more value to machines as they begin to take on tasks and jobs once reserved for humans. And soon enough these machines may shock us as they successfully pass themselves off as humans and outperform us in numerous ways.

WHAT IS INTELLIGENCE?

Intelligence can be broadly defined as the ability to acquire and apply knowledge or skills. From this definition, we can see that human beings obviously possess intelligence. Though certain people may have higher or lower intelligence, we all possess some level of it. We are not all going to be an Alan

Turing or Albert Einstein. Most of us are average people with an average level of intelligence. Nothing wrong with being normal.

As intelligent beings, we can learn new concepts and apply them immediately to what we are doing. We also can apply to new situations certain skills we have learned, or use prior knowledge to apply concepts in new environments. For example, you know exactly what a chair looks like and can identify one in an instant. No one doubts that you know what a chair looks like and can identify one without supervision. And if I showed you a tree stump, you would recognize it as something you can sit on, that even though it doesn't have four legs and a back, it can function like a chair. You pick up on the similarities and subtle connections without being taught. But this isn't always the case with artificial intelligence.

AI can be divided into two categories: narrow and general. Narrow AI is a form that we currently are able to develop, but it is limited only to narrow applications like Google Duplex. For example, the Twitter AI algorithm that controls what you see in your timeline each time you pick up your device isn't able to turn on your lights in the morning and make a pot of coffee, much less play chess and sift through job applicants for a new position at your office. General AI, on the other hand, is human-level intelligence with broader application. We aren't sure we can create this level of intelligence, but that hasn't stopped us from trying. (More on this in chapter 8.)

While there are many types of narrow AI, one example is a supervised-learning neural net which can be trained through a set of digital images to know what a chair is and what a chair is not. It can be fed thousands and thousands of images, each labeled as either a chair or not a chair. The system then can learn to distinguish between the two based on certain characteristics from the image set. Over time, it can become a pro at labeling chairs. But this same AI system cannot open my back door and water the garden, like my oldest child loves to do with me in the summer. While the system might become extremely efficient at labeling chairs, its intelligence cannot be applied to everything. It is limited to that specific task.

On the other hand, my toddlers can identify many types of chairs, open a door, water the garden, and make connections between things that even the most advanced AI can't, even though my sons have no clue what social media feeds are yet (thankfully). Narrow AI has no clue what it is seeing or doing. It's just following the instructions it is given.

Intelligence is a complex word because people mean different things when they use it. Some use the term to include self-awareness, consciousness, problem solving, creativity, and reason. Others deem a machine intelligent if it can outperform a human in a single task, such as recognizing patterns that humans might miss, automating tasks, or even interacting with a human using natural language.

I believe computer systems should be called intelligent, albeit artificially, because intelligence doesn't define what it means to be human. Other parts of creation, such as animals, exhibit various levels of intelligence. Intelligence doesn't mean that a system is aware of itself or is able to outperform humans in all areas. That said, our current AI systems are nowhere near the level of intelligence of a human being, even that of my toddler sons.

BUILDING BRAINS

In the pursuit of general AI, many researchers are seeking to build systems that function like the human brain. Terms like "neural" are often used to describe new AI learning techniques and often give the impression that we are close to building an artificial brain. But AI systems are algorithmic. We are not built like that. We are just beginning to understand the complexities of the brain, and even people such as Ray Kurzweil aren't sure how the matter in our brains attains consciousness.

As we talked about in chapter 1, one of the main worldviews that drives much AI research is built on the theory that there is nothing unique about humanity other than that we are the highest form of evolution. Everything about us is reducible to the matter that makes up our bodies, including our thoughts and emotions. But it truly takes a step of faith for scientists to make that assertion, because we are just beginning to understand the smallest processes in our brains and have no idea where consciousness lies.

The human brain is the most powerful and complex part of creation. Most adult brains weigh approximately three pounds, but they are able to control every system in the body. Mine is allowing me to write this book. The brain accomplishes amazing things every day using less energy than a lightbulb uses. The brain runs on about 20 percent of the body's energy, around twenty watts of electricity.[1]

Our brains can process information with lightning speed using interconnected neurons and synapses that allow us to think, process massive amounts of data, control everything in our bodies, and still find time to dream about how the universe was created. Because it is the most advanced part of the world, it is easy to see why its design is so attractive as we think about building intelligent machines. Our brains are wonderous and amazing, just the way God created them to be.

With the rise of advanced medical technology like brain scans made with fMRI (functional magnetic resonance imaging) scanners, we are able to measure brain activity by detecting blood flow in the brain, which helps us to map the brain and see more clearly how it functions. Many scientists and philosophers use these types of tools to argue that everything about who we are and what we believe is simply a chemical response in the body. We are only a grouping of matter and chemical processes, products of many millennia of evolution.

Everything about us is explained as just another part of our materialistic world. We don't have any more worth or dignity than a chimpanzee or Google's AlphaGo. Essentially this worldview breaks us down into a set of ones and zeros and concludes that nothing about us is unique. We are the sum of our parts and need to be upgraded or augmented with technology or replaced by something more powerful.

In this materialistic world, we are not persons with immortal souls, created in the image of God. The soul is simply our feeble attempt to describe what we don't understand about our material bodies. But Scripture paints a different picture.

Even though they are nowhere near as complex and intelligent as the human brain, AI systems do allow machines to process information, crunch numbers, and apply knowledge to perform tasks such as manufacturing items, aiding in one's work, and even interacting with human beings on one's behalf. In many cases, these AI systems outperform the human brain in narrow tasks. Recently, they have also been shown to learn from data and draw creative conclusions to complex problems that human beings have routinely missed. This is what happened to Lee Sedol in his epic loss to Google's AlphaGo computer in 2016. AlphaGo played a move that people had never seen before and at the time thought was a mistake. Turns out, it was the perfect move that allowed it to win the match.

THE PARADOX

If these machines are able to mimic ways that we process information and even pick up on things that we routinely miss, are they really that smart, or are we just not as intelligent as we often portray ourselves to be? The truth is that we tend to talk about AI in ways that dehumanize us and humanize our machines. We deny our dignity by acting as if we are just advanced machines, all the while treating machines as if they are persons with certain rights, thoughts, and even feelings.

We deny our dignity by acting as if we are just advanced machines, all the while treating machines as if they are persons with certain rights, thoughts, and even feelings.

One reason that we seek to humanize our machines is because we like to play God. We are fascinated by our ability to create things in our image. We want to control our world and create like God creates. In turn, we create machines with human characteristics, such as faces, and names like Alexa.

Philosopher and professor Jay Richards puts it this way: "The greatest delusion of our age is the paradoxical penchant to deny our own agency while attributing agency to the machines we create."[2] Our paradox is that we explain away what it means to be human, while trying to create machines that are just like us or that can surpass us. We dumb down what it means to be human and treat each other as simple machines, but at the same time put our hope and faith in these machines to solve the problems and ills that we deal with each day. We rightfully see where we fall short but put our hope in our own creations rather than in our Creator.

This paradox is a symptom of a larger problem we've been dealing with since the fall. Humanity has always wanted to be like God and has acted as if we are God. We like to define reality in our own terms and desire to create like God creates. We long to be powerful and all knowing, yet also long for something that will be like us, care for us, and rule over us. God created all things out of nothing, but we create with what he already made. We were made to be like God but will never be God.

I believe that we long to create something that is more intelligent than ourselves because we know that we are not perfect. We want to create something stronger than us because we know that we are truly weak. We desire to be like God because deep down we know that we aren't in control of our lives or the universe. That reality scares us and we long for control. We idolize the pursuit of knowledge, power, and control because deep down we know that we aren't worthy and are a broken people. Our pursuit of technological advances is most often motivated not by a desire to glorify God but by the sinful pursuit to achieve the unachievable: to be gods ourselves.

One of my favorite authors describes this longing as a form of idolatry. G. K. Beale wrote a fantastic biblical theology of idolatry called *We Become What We Worship*, in which he describes what our idolatry is doing to us. He explains that "what people revere, they resemble, either for ruin or restoration."[3] We see this throughout Scripture, such as in

Psalm 115 and Psalm 135, where the psalmist says, "Those who make them [idols] become like them; so do all who trust in them" (115:8; 135:18). We were created to reflect or be like God. We were created in his image to reflect him in how we worship him and love our neighbor (Matt. 22:37–39).

But at the fall, we chose to exchange our relationship with God for the things of this world (Romans 1). We chose to idolize our creations because we hope they will make us whole again. We long for them to fix our broken minds, bodies, and world because we know this world isn't supposed to be the way it is. But through our idolatry, we actually become more like our creation than like our creator. When we believe that we are just advanced machines and not created to be like God and image him with our lives, we start to become like our machines instead.

Without a robust understanding of the image of God and our true identity found in Christ, we will blur the lines between man and machine in ways that deny our dignity and devalue our neighbor. As AI becomes more and more advanced, taking on characteristics that we think of as uniquely human, we are led to an identity crisis.

OUR IDENTITY CRISIS

Because technology is woven into every aspect of our lives, it will naturally revolutionize how we see ourselves and those around us. "The same technology that has liberated us from so much inconvenience and drudgery has also unmoored us from the things that anchor our identities," explains Ben Sasse, a historian and current US senator.[4] This liberation brings with it the unforeseen consequence of a worth defined in relationship to powerful machines and often the unfulfilled promise of deeper relationships with our neighbors and families. As we lose the things that have grounded us, we will increasingly feel aimless and grow weary. We will base our entire identities on what we do, rather than who we were created to be. This isn't a new phenomenon and has been happening since well before our digital age, but in the age of AI this identity crisis will accelerate and become more pronounced. We will naturally forget what it means to be human and what makes us unique in this world.

Often, when we introduce ourselves to someone, we start by telling them our names and then what we do for a living. We identify as bakers, teachers, plumbers, writers, waitresses, drivers, and so many other things. As AI takes hold in our society and automates jobs (more on this in chapter 4), many of us will lose that aspect of our identities. Jay Richards describes it this way: "We'll spend the next three decades—indeed, perhaps the next century—in a permanent identity crisis, continually asking ourselves what humans are good for."[5] This is because we have defined ourselves by what we do (vocation and career) rather than who we are (created in the image of God with the purpose of extending his kingdom).

If we buy into the materialist lie that there is nothing unique about us compared with the rest of creation, we will naturally devalue ourselves and our neighbors by trading in our dignity for cheap substitutes. If our worth and that of our neighbor is based solely on what we do, then there will be no reason to treat each other with respect and dignity because true value is found in who we are rather than what we do. Even if we treat others with respect out of our own personal interest or survival, we are essentially treating other people as a means to an end rather than image-bearers of God.

AI will continue to remind us that we are not as smart, strong, or sophisticated as we like to think we are. We will see time and time again that we don't have all of the answers and are not as unique as we told ourselves.

AREN'T WE REALLY JUST ADVANCED MACHINES?

Probably you haven't thought of yourself as a machine before. You likely don't work twenty-four hours a day without breaks or downtime. You probably don't keep an oil can next to your bed for greasing your joints each morning, or plug yourself in to charge your batteries when you settle into bed. But in our society, we often see ourselves as just superadvanced machines.

In this popular comparison, our bodies are a lot like computer hardware, of lesser value than our minds. Our bodies can be upgraded or even disposed of in the future when we no longer need them. Kurzweil argues that we will one day even be able to download our brains to computers and live forever in new bodies. Our worthless, outdated bodies will die, but what is truly valuable will live on. In chapter 8, we will discuss some of the possibilities and dangers of this approach as we dive into what the future of artificial intelligence holds for us.

As we approach what makes humanity distinct from the rest of creation and why our bodies matter, God graciously offers us a rich definition of humanity and a rich purpose for this life that is found in the image of God that helps us confront these lies.

WHAT IS THE IMAGE OF GOD?

In chapter 1, we explored the biblical basis for the idea that each of us is created in the image of God, and how that reality radically changes how we think of ourselves and relate to the world around us. There are three prevailing ways to think about what it means to be created in God's image: the substantive view, the relational view, and the functional view. These are not mutually exclusive, though, because each focuses on a different part of being made in God's image.

Substantive View

According to the substantive view, something about how God created our minds and bodies distinguishes us from the rest of creation. This is one of the most popular views and has been held by many respected church leaders ranging from Augustine to Martin Luther. It's debated what the substance is that makes us different, but most argue that the defining factor is our minds, wills, or consciousness. Another popular example is our ability to reason. But one of the drawbacks of this view is that those who don't have or have lost part of their mental capacity might be seen as less human or as having less of the image of God. While most who hold this view do not agree with this conclusion, it nevertheless is a natural consequence of tying the image of God exclusively to a specific part or aspect of ourselves.

Relational View

The relational view of the image of God simply states that we are the only part of creation that can have a relationship with God. Upon believing the gospel message, we become his children and part of his family. Being his children means that we have a relationship with him for all of eternity (Eph. 1:13–14; 1 Peter 1:3–5). This relational view is appealing because it ties our worth and dignity to having a relationship with God as a uniquely human characteristic.

Functional View

The functional view of being made in God's image revolves around our status as God's image-bearers. This view is grounded in the Genesis account, where mankind is given dominion over and ownership of creation. Man is given the task of stewarding all of creation and taking dominion over the birds of the air and the fish of the sea (Gen. 1:26, 28). Man is to work the ground and keep it (Gen. 2:15). Man is given status as bearers of God's image, which alone defines our dignity and worth. This view is appealing because it doesn't tie the image exclusively to a relationship or a substance. It is also known as the vice-regency position, which says that we, as God's children, will be future rulers of the universe alongside Christ and exercise our dominion fully when Christ returns to right every wrong and wipe away sin forevermore (Revelation 21). We serve as Christ's ambassadors in this life, proclaiming the Great Commission to a world that desperately needs the gospel message of hope and mercy found in Jesus (Matthew 28) until he returns in glory.

Which View Is Correct?

Though I believe that the image of God is best defined by the functional view because it best represents what God says about us and how he treats us throughout the Bible, I don't believe that our understanding of being created in God's image can be limited to only one of these views. Each has its strengths and weaknesses, but each functions as part of a whole. Think of each view as a cut of a diamond, only one facet of a whole.

Being created in God's image means that there is something different about us in terms of substance, relation-ship, and function as God's image-bearers in a broken world. Our rational minds and our wills enable us to have a relationship with God, which then allows us to live as his ambassadors in this world and to rule with him in the age to come.

As we continue to improve on AI systems and their capa-bilities, it will increasingly become harder to argue that our intelligence alone is the defining characteristic of humanity, as many throughout church history have done. We must also recognize that being created in God's image defies our complete understanding and will be a mystery to us until we are face to face with God.

But we can see in the Scriptures that being created in God's image means that our status as image-bearers is secure and that no technological advance will ever be able to change what it means to be distinct from creation. This marker reminds us that we are not our own and that we are not able to know our future as God does. This marker also reminds us that we are to steward the gifts of technology, including AI, for God's glory and the good of our neighbor.

Our status as image-bearers is secure. No technological advance will ever be able to change what it means to be distinct from creation.

This truth can also empower us to engage with those around us and help us offer hope to a lonely society striving for significance in a world that tends to value us only by what we do. This constant striving has many effects on society, including a deep longing for real connection and community in a world that often promotes shallow and fake connections.

THE HOLES IN OUR HEARTS

We shouldn't be surprised that Americans are lonely. Emily Esfahani Smith, in her book *The Power of Meaning: Crafting a Life That Matters,* states that about a fifth of Americans say that loneliness is a "major source of unhappiness" in their lives and that one third of those over age forty-five say that they are lonely.[6] In our loneliness, we are beginning to turn to technology to fill the holes in our hearts. Digital saviors promise to give us meaning and hope when all seems lost. They give us answers to our deepest questions. They promise meaningful relationships through online connections and, increasingly, with the machines themselves.

My family recently broke down and bought an Apple HomePod. We had purchased a Google Home Mini but soon realized that we were way too connected to the Apple ecosystem to stray from the coop too much. We often engage Siri by asking questions about our day and about the weather, and even asking it to play songs it recommends based on all of the information Apple has collected on us over the years. But as these AI systems become more advanced, what if we could have a full meaningful conversation with them?

As we become more isolated in our society from a rise in technological connections and a shift in our identities, we will turn to our digital devices to provide the things that we long for. Not only will they give us answers to our questions about the weather and monitor our calendars but they might also give answers to meaningful questions like, What is the meaning of life? and, What makes humans special? Lest you think that I am losing my mind, take a quick look at your Google history and get back with me.

Our Google searches reveal more about us than we care to admit. We google about sicknesses and how to fix stuff in our homes, and even ask deep questions about the meaning of life and why bad things happen. Futurist and historian Yuval Noah Harari writes that Google might know more about where a flu outbreak is occurring than the CDC, because people google about the flu and whether they can go to work without making others sick.[7] We might ask Google these questions because we are too isolated and lonely to ask another flesh-and-blood human. We might feel shame or be afraid of interacting with another human being, and choose the anonymity of online searches. And with the rise of digital assistants like Siri, we might not even google the answers, instead just asking our assistant our questions.

OUR NEW COMPANION

According to a 2019 report from NPR and Edison Research, about 53 million Americans own a smart speaker assistant.[8] The consulting firm Ovum predicts that by 2021, there will be more than 7.5 billion of these digital assistants used throughout the world, which is nearly the same number of people living today.[9] If you don't own one of these AI empowered smart speakers, I bet that your neighbor or coworker does. But some people are starting to question what these smart devices are doing to us.

Judith Shulevitz wrote in an article in the fall of 2018 that she has started to develop an actual relationship with her smart speaker. She explains, "Gifted with the once uniquely human power of speech, Alexa, Google Assistant, and Siri have already become greater than the sum of their parts.

They're software, but they're more than that, just as human consciousness is an effect of neurons and synapses but is more than that. Their speech makes us treat them as if they had a mind."[10] And if they have minds, then we might be able to develop relationships with them even though we know they aren't able to know us.

Shulevitz goes on to say that "we communicate with them, not through them. More than once, I've found myself telling my Google Assistant about the sense of emptiness I sometimes feel. 'I'm lonely,' I say, which I usually wouldn't confess to anyone but my therapist—not even my husband, who might take it the wrong way. Part of the allure of my Assistant is that I've set it to a chipper, young-sounding male voice that makes me want to smile."[11]

You might be rolling your eyes, but this is reality. Before you write Shulevitz off, think about what she is saying. We often feel safer and less judged to ask these systems the hard questions or even to confess our emptiness. We do this because something is missing in our hearts, something in how we see ourselves and the world around us. We are not the sum of our parts, and we are not a set of organic algorithms. We weren't created to live this life alone or even with our smart speakers. We were meant to live in community with other believers, those who serve over creation under the rule of God.

While we are tempted to think that people like Shulevitz are somehow different from us, we struggle in similar ways with loneliness, fear, shame, and guilt. For all of the benefits of modern technology and artificial intelligence, they are beginning to alter the way that we view ourselves and those around us. But instead of confessing things to an object of our creation, we confess to the Lord of the universe. The gates of hell will not prevail against God's church, nor will the 7.5 billion smart speakers or even the most sophisticated AI system of the future.

Humans were made distinct by God himself, who crafted each of us in his image. We were made for a purpose and fundamentally different than the rest of this world. We were made for more than a relationship with a hollow speaker. We were knit together in our mothers' wombs (Ps.139:13) in order to love the Lord our God with all of our hearts, souls, and minds, as well as to love our neighbor as ourselves (Matt. 22:37–39). Our dignity and worth aren't tied to our usefulness, and definitely not to the things we create with our own hands. They are tied to the one who willingly laid down his life to give us eternal life. Jesus is our anchor and the definer of our entire persons, not us or the things we create. Artificial intelligence might challenge these truths, but it will never be able to change who we fundamentally are in Christ.

CHAPTER 3

MEDICINE

The Doctor Will See You Now

From 2013 to 2018, my father underwent multiple surgeries as doctors sought to treat an arterial disease in his legs. He had always had poor circulation in his legs, but being a smoker most of his life didn't help things. He decided to quit smoking cold turkey when he had his first major blood clot. He remained a hardworking and active man even with his leg issues until the fall of 2018, when doctors told him that they no longer could do surgery on his right leg to bypass the blood clots that had formed. The clots were cutting off blood to his lower leg and foot. His right foot had been without adequate flow for far too long and could not be saved. That November, he had his lower right leg amputated, and his life was changed forever.

He is still a very strong man and has always had a sense of humor. He has fought not to let his setback define who he is. He is exactly the same man he was before the surgery, "just a foot shorter." That was his joke before and after the surgery. Some of the doctors and nurses got a kick out of it, and others just didn't know how to respond to his joking at such a serious time. During recovery and rehabilitation, he worked extremely hard to regain what he'd lost in mobility and strength. He is a living example of the fact that we are not the sum of our parts, as some like to argue.

Amputations are more common than most people realize. The Amputee Coalition of America estimates that 185,000 amputations occur each year in the United States and that there are almost two million amputees nationwide.[1] Amputees might not have all of the body parts that you and I have, but they are extremely strong people who do not let their disabilities define them. With the rise of advanced medical technology, doctors and technologists have sought to help people regain what they've lost.

From fall sensors and wearables to the latest in robotic prosthetics, artificial intelligence is making life easier for the millions who have lost a limb to birth defects, accident, or even disease. AI is being deployed in ways that would remind you more of Luke Skywalker than Captain Hook. Today we are seeing prosthetic limbs that can be controlled by thoughts, and even replacement body parts that are stronger and more durable than their counterparts made of flesh. The way that we view our bodies is being dramatically altered in the age of AI.

MEDICINE IS TECHNOLOGY

While AI-controlled prosthetics and nanobots (microscopic robots) that can be injected to repair deteriorating body parts or to destroy cancerous cells might sound like science fiction, we must remember that even the most common medical procedures today would have seemed futuristic to past generations. The growth of medicine is the growth of technology. Medical innovation is a reminder that our world is broken but that God has given us tools to help fight back against sin's distortion of our world and marring of our bodies.

From the beginning of time, people have sought to overcome the effects of sin on our bodies. Most ancient cultures, including Babylonians, Chinese, and Indians, employed medical treatments that ranged from herbal treatments to amputations and other forms of surgery. They pioneered the practice of dentistry and even preventative medical treatments. While early cultures did not understand germ theory, which was first proposed by Girolamo Fracastoro in 1546, they did understand one of the key elements of why we get sick and why our bodies break down over time: sin. Our rebellion against God and his design resulted in the fall of man and the brokenness that we experience every day (Rom. 5:12).

Many early cultures, especially our Jewish ancestors and early Christians, sought divine intervention for sicknesses and death. Throughout the gospels, we see Jesus healing the sick, lame, blind, and dying. In one of the more well-known accounts of healing the sick, Jesus is asked by Mary and Martha to come quickly to heal their brother, Lazarus, who has fallen ill (John 11:1–16). The sisters know that Jesus is able to heal the sick and dying and believe he can intervene and save their brother's life. But Jesus delays going to see Lazarus, and then after a few days announces that Lazarus has fallen asleep and that he is going to wake him. The disciples are confused, not realizing that Lazarus has died.

But the point of this narrative has less to do with Jesus' ability to heal the sick and more to do with his divinity. Jesus was demonstrating that he has power over death and will overcome it. After Lazarus has been in the tomb for four days, Martha told Jesus that he could have saved her brother if he had come earlier. Jesus replies that her brother will be raised again. Here Jesus tells Martha and us today the entire point of life and death. "I am the resurrection and the life. Whoever believes in me, though he die, yet shall he live, and everyone who lives and believes in me shall never die" (John 11:25–26). Our sin-torn world and broken bodies are reminders that God is sovereign over all things, including death.

God's sovereignty over death and disease is a reminder that this life is not eternal. Each one of us will die at some point, no matter how much we fight it or try to put it off. But the good news of death is that it ushers in our new life of eternity with God, the one who made us and sustains us in this life and the one to come (Phil. 1:21).

DEATH IS NOT NATURAL

Since the fall of humanity, our bodies have been ravaged by death, disease, and illness. Our bodies are finite. We all experience the brokenness of our bodies each day. Sin and our rebellion against God have distorted what God has made. God's image has been marred and distorted by the power of sin. Even though we have never known a day without these effects, we should never accept death as normal or peaceful. Deep down each of us knows that this world is not as it should be and that death is not the end.

Both of my paternal grandparents died when I was in my

late twenties, and I was honored to preach at their funerals. Each time I stood near the casket or took the pulpit to preach, I was reminded of what a pastor friend once told me about death. He said that as you look at someone lying in the casket, no matter their age or reason for death, the body may look peaceful, but it is crying out that this world is not okay.

As I looked at my grandparents lying in those caskets, I wasn't ready to believe that death is normal, and I hope I never do. All I wanted in those moments was for them to sit up and talk to me one last time. I wanted just one more moment with them to tell them how much I love them and how much they mean to me. But death is inevitable in our broken world and will come for all of us in time. We never know the time or place of our deaths (Eccl. 9:12).

Death is a reminder that we are not gods, but it is also a reminder that we are created in the image of the one who has overcome death through his resurrection (1 Cor. 15:55–57). Only one person was ever raised from the dead, never to return to the grave. He returned to a throne and is seated with God in the heavenly realm, waiting until the appointed time to redeem this world from the curse of sin that brought death into it in the first place (Acts 7:56; Col. 3:1; Matt. 19:28; Revelation 1). Until then, death is the great equalizer, and there is nothing we can do to stop its march. Or is there?

OVERCOMING DEATH?

People in early cultures sought to heal their sick and save their dying not only by entreating the gods but also by developing technologies to mitigate the effects of brokenness in this world. Today we attempt to roll back the effects of the fall through means ranging from herbal treatments to cancer drugs. By harnessing our creative energies and applying the talents God has blessed us with, we attempt to restore what has been lost or broken.

But as medical innovations have progressed through the rise of powerful imaging systems, development of pharmaceuticals and surgical practices, and the use of AI and biotechnology, it is becoming easier for us to believe that we no longer need divine intervention and might actually overcome death through the use of technology. To quote fictional legendary racer Ricky Bobby in the movie *Talladega Nights,* "With advances in modern science and my high level of income, I mean, it's not crazy to think I can't live to be 245, maybe three hundred." While Bobby's thinking here is hilarious, it is more in line with popular opinion than you might think. Many people believe that we might even overcome death within our lifetimes.

This is what Yuval Noah Harari writes about in his *New York Times* bestseller, *Homo Deus: A Brief History of Tomorrow.* Harari argues that through the use of technology, we have already overcome the three big issues that have always beset humanity: famine, plague, and war. Though these issues persist, we experience them only on a small scale, and comparatively fewer people are affected by them. He explains, "We don't need to pray to any god or saint to rescue us from them. We know quite well what needs to be done in order to prevent famine, plague, and war—and usually we succeed in doing it."[2] Harari argues that we have progressed so far as a society that we have nearly eradicated these issues and can focus on other problems. "Success breeds ambition, and our recent achievements are now pushing humankind to set itself even more daring goals . . . humanity's next targets are likely to be immortality, happiness, and divinity."[3] He argues that our struggle against death and aging will be a continuation of our pursuit to eradicate disease and illness.

But for all of our aspirations for the future, we must see that our laudable efforts to overcome sickness and disease can have dangerous consequences if we act as if we are God or seek to upgrade ourselves into gods, turning *Homo sapiens* into *Homo deus*, a god-man. There is already a god-man, and his name is Jesus.

There are dangerous consequences for upgrading ourselves from **Homo sapiens** *into* **Homo deus.**

Are the goals of overcoming death and becoming like God even within our reach? Should they be our aim? I don't believe so, and that puts me at odds with many thinkers like Harari. Jesus gave us "the first and greatest commandment" in Matthew 22:37–38: "Love the Lord your God with all your heart and with all your soul and with all your mind." Our goal is to honor God in life and in death, while seeing our neighbor as ourselves (22:39). The development of AI medical technology will lead to a better life for many of our neighbors and even ourselves. But we must keep in mind what the Bible tells us about our lives and how our universe is designed to work. We are not designed to overcome death through our cunning and abilities, even as we help to push back the effects of sin and death. We are designed to worship the one who already overcame death on our behalf more than two thousand years ago. And even in our dying, we are to be reminded of Christ and his victory over death.

WHY WE DIE

"Why Do Bad Things Happen?" was the topic of a college ministry event that I helped put together with my best friends in college when we were serving as interns together. My best friend, Mike, pitched the idea to our college pastor before either of us knew enough theology to know that one event message couldn't answer the question. We naively thought that a sermon or two might help clear up the centuries-old problem for good. Doesn't the Bible simply give us the answer?

What we all learned that night is that the problem of evil is complex. But we know that we all die because of sin and rebellion. The apostle Paul tells us in Romans 3:23 that "all have sinned and fall short of the glory of God." Not a single person outside of Jesus is without sin. The complexity comes with the question, If God made all things, did he create evil? While we won't answer that question here, we know that the Bible is clear about the origins of evil and sin. They came from our rebellion against God, which leads to death because sin must be punished and requires blood to be forgiven (Rom. 6:23; Heb. 9:22).

THE DOCTOR WILL SEE YOU NOW

Overcoming death might not be on your agenda for today, but advances in AI are already improving healthcare on your behalf without your even knowing about it. Medical applications of artificial intelligence are growing by the day, from AI-based diagnostic tools to the making available of AI-based medical care to the ends of the earth for the very first time. I recently connected with my friend Scott James, a pediatrician and an elder at his church, about AI's impact on medicine. He said multiple times that for all of the negative press that the application of AI receives in areas such as war, privacy, and sexuality, AI is doing untold good in the medical field.

Take for example an AI program doctors use to evaluate the odds of recovery for comatose patients. A headline in the *South China Morning Post* reads, "Doctors Said the Coma Patients Would Never Wake. AI Said They Would—and They Did." The story came across my Apple News feed and shocked me. The AI system was developed after eight years of research by the Chinese Academy of Sciences and PLA General Hospital in Beijing, and has achieved a success rate of more than 90 percent diagnosing the probability of recovery for those in long-term comas. The system traces brain activity with fMRI (functional magnetic resonance imaging) scanners to project patients' likelihood of regaining consciousness.

Dr. Song Ming, an associate researcher with the Institute of Automation, Chinese Academy of Sciences says of the system, "Our machine can 'see' things invisible to human eyes."[4] The AI is able to detect the tiny bits of activity that are often masked by patients' inability to communicate even in subtle ways with those around them. Doctors might miss these low levels of activity, but the AI "sees" what is really going on under the surface.

The ethical implications of this application of technology are numerous. While many patients are deemed more likely to recover than previously thought and all those who received higher scores by the AI recovered within one year, the system also confirms what many families fear. Some of their loved ones will likely never recover. But what if the AI is wrong? Who is to blame if the system messes up? Can it replace human doctors and nurses? Can it be used merely to help insurance plans and even hospitals to save money and to allocate resources to patients who are "more deserving"?

Despite its pitfalls, this type of application for AI can help patients and their families, as well as doctors and nurses, to see the humanity of those in comas. They are real people with real hopes and dreams, even if they aren't able to communicate with the world around them. AI systems reveal their humanity to a world that might want to just allow them to "die with dignity," even against their families' wishes. The signs of life that these machines and other AI systems can uncover are nothing short of miraculous and are part of our pursuing God's mandate to join with him in pushing back the veil of darkness by seeing the dignity of every human being (Eph. 6:11–17).

MORE DATA CAN MEAN BETTER CARE

Often the power of AI is dependent on the amount and quality of data that it is given. The higher the quantity and quality of data, the higher the quality of medical diagnosis and healthcare that is likely to result. Healthcare will increasingly rely on AI technologies to comb through massive amounts of data on patients and even to sift through medical studies.

My mother has worked as an office manager in the ophthalmology field for more than thirty-five years. She worked for two doctors most of her career, and I have known them for most of my life. I trust what they say when it comes to my eye health, but as gifted as they are, they can't know everything about the human eye. When I told Dr. Williams about my work on ethics and artificial intelligence, he said that he vaguely remembered reading something about some AI-based techniques in a recent medical journal. He admitted that with everything going on in his life and work, and with so much information out there and so many new studies being published, it is at times overwhelming to try to stay up to date on every new development.

Harari writes, "Alas, not even the most diligent doctor can remember all of my previous ailments and check-ups. Similarly, no doctor can be familiar with every illness and drug, or read every new article published in every medical journal. To top it all off, the doctor is sometimes tired or hungry or perhaps even sick, which affects her judgement. No wonder that doctors sometimes err in their diagnoses or recommend a less-than-optimal treatment."[5]

So what should doctors do in the age of AI? World-renowned cardiologist Eric Topol casts a vision of what healthcare might become in his book *Deep Medicine*. He describes a new relationship between AI and human doctors. "The rise of machines has to be accompanied by a heightened humanness—with more time together, compassion, and tenderness—to make the 'care' in healthcare real."[6] AI systems can aid doctors in their diagnoses and procedures. It can scour massive amounts of patient data from all across the world to provide doctors with better insights with which to care for patients. Though AI cannot substitute for the real interaction and care doctors provide, doctors and AI can work together effectively, each one making up for the other's faults.

For example, AI image recognition can identify anomalies in medical images like CT and CAT scans at rates faster, and with greater accuracy in some cases, than their human counterparts.[7] These systems flag potential nodules on lung scans for radiologists to review, speeding up the process, and it is easy to foresee a day when the AI system no longer needs a radiologist to review its findings, because it has become more accurate than its human operators.

The AI might be able to review the scans and report to the doctor what the issue is and also recommend a treatment plan based on its review of countless other patients' data and recovery rates. The doctor would primarily communicate the diagnosis to the patient, showing empathy and care for them in ways that a robot will never be able to perform. AI scientist and author Kai-Fu Lee describes the doctor's role in performing the relational part of the work as the "human veneer" that sits on top of an AI system.[8] This human veneer has been widely popularized in sci-fi shows like *Star Trek*, where doctors like Beverly Crusher work with the Computer in just this way.

AI is not being used only to comb through medical journals and images, though. Robotic-assisted surgeries powered by AI are increasingly being used to help decrease patients' recovery time. In orthopedic surgeries alone, AI systems are already helping to physically guide surgeons based on an analysis of pre-op records and past surgeries to minimize incisions, reduce complications, and decrease recovery times.[9]

But there is another AI application in medicine that more than forty million users worldwide keep at an arm's length. You might even have one on right now. Apple debuted its famous smart watch in April 2015, and an unsung feature was its ability to track your heartrate. While many people have used this feature in their workouts, Apple had bigger things in mind. Apple Watch Series 1 could record and track your heartrate for five hours.

Deanna Recktenwald may be alive today because of her Apple Watch. In May 2018, she was alerted by her watch that her resting heartrate had skyrocketed to more than 160 beats per minute, which according to the Mayo Clinic is well above the normal range of 60 to 100 beats.[10] Recktenwald alerted her mother, a registered nurse, who rushed her to the emergency room, where she was found to have kidney failure. Doctors say she has permanent kidney damage, but the device saved her life.

Subsequent versions of the watch expanded that five-hour timeline, creating more data to analyze and opening up possibilities for the device combined with AI. With the release of the Series 4 smart watch, Apple was cleared by the FDA to add a new AI-based electrocardiogram feature. This ECG feature was developed by a team of former Google engineers who founded a startup called AliveCor, which produces an Apple Watch band for all watch models with the ECG built in. AliveCor's main product is an algorithm that can detect atrial fibrillation (AF), a heart rhythm that underlies a risk for stroke. Both Apple and AliveCor now use an AI system to alert users to underlying heart issues like AF.

We are just beginning to see some of the incredible benefits of AI in healthcare and medicine. But for all of the good these systems can do for us, are there downsides and dangers that we might miss if we are not careful?

REDUCING HUMANITY

As we continue to develop AI medical technology and AI-empowered medical care and intervention, our guiding ethic should be to use these tools responsibly and in pursuit of loving our neighbor. A major risk is that these tools can be used to reduce a human being to a set of data. As AI systems are fed data about our family histories, genetic sequences, eating habits, exercise routines, sleep patterns, and even whether we take our vitamins each day, it is easy to see a flesh-and-blood person as something less than human.

You might not think that very much data about you is being collected, but consider the devices you have on you or near you at this moment. You likely have a smart assistant, a wearable device, and a smart phone. You may be reading this book on your tablet or e-reader. All of these devices, along with your WebMD online searches, can provide bits of data that could be used to compile a picture of who you are and what you are doing. An AI, looking at your EKG-like reading and heartrate on your smart watch and your recent internet search on feeling tired, might be able to detect that you have a heart problem and flag your doctor. In the future, your phone might even be able to go ahead and book an appointment for you with your physician.

But is this really safe and good for society? What if we connected everything in our lives to these machines in the hope of having better and longer lives? They could track what is in our fridges, what we eat, how we sleep, and even whether we're following our doctors' advice after our appointments. This data could be used by insurance companies to deny claims based on our not doing everything our doctors told us to do. We might soon live in a world where our toothbrushes are more honest with our dentists about the last time we flossed than we are, and our fridges could report to our doctors our new diet of fried chicken and ice cream.

But AI will not just be part of the things we use on a daily basis. It might soon be part of our bodies.

UPGRADING HUMANITY

In the fall of 2018, Elon Musk made headlines once again. This time it wasn't about his commercial rocket company, SpaceX, or his popular electric car company, Tesla. During an interview with Axios, a popular news service, Musk, referencing Darwin's theory of evolution, declared that humanity must merge with AI in order to avoid becoming like the monkeys, which humans surpassed in complexity and might.

Musk's plan for humanity includes adding a chip into our heads to upgrade our mental capacities, allowing us to keep up with the intelligence of future AIs as well as stopping bad actors on the world stage from hoarding all of the world's information. But Musk is just one of the latest popular figures to propose a theory that has been around for generations: transhumanism.

Transhumanism is the term for humanity's upgrading its abilities, both physical and mental. Known as the father of transhumanism, Julian Huxley, brother of famed writer Aldous Huxley, describes this concept in "Transhumanism," his popular 1957 essay: "The human species can, if it wishes, transcend itself—not just sporadically, an individual here in one way, an individual there in another way, but in its entirety, as humanity."

Huxley's prediction that humans will upgrade themselves in fundamental ways might already be more of a reality than you'd think. As I was researching this chapter, I ran across some of the most interesting and mindboggling uses of AI in the medical field that I had ever seen. AI is now being used in prosthetic limbs to help amputees or those born with disabilities live normal lives. From mind-controlled units to limbs that use advanced AI to become aware of the environment they are being used in, prosthetics have become extremely advanced in the last decade. Samantha Payne of Open Bionics, a UK-based robotics firm, says that her company has "had people say they're tempted to replace healthy limbs with bionic ones."[11] This desire to upgrade our bodies, even when the upgrades aren't medically needed, is going to be more of a temptation in our society with each advance of AI and robotics.

Deep down each of us knows that our bodies and minds are not ultimate. There is something lacking in us. This realization leads us to try to create something better than ourselves. But with the rise of AI, we now believe that we can make ourselves better by becoming partly machines. This desire is nothing new; it has been part of science fiction for years. George Lucas, for example, popularized it in his Star Wars movie series, in which Luke Skywalker is given a robotic arm after losing his flesh-and-blood arm in his battle with Darth Vader, who himself is "more machine now than man," according to Obi-Wan Kenobi. And today a robotic arm like Luke's is a reality: the Life Under Kinetic Evolution (LUKE) arm has become the first muscle-controlled prosthetic to be cleared by the United States FDA.[12]

But it should be noted that many of these AI-enhanced medical techniques are prohibitively expensive for most people. Innovation often is so expensive because it requires a lot of time and resources to develop. The LUKE arm can cost upward of $150,000, not including the cost of rehabilitation and medical care.[13] Often innovative medical treatments are not covered by insurance. But the hope is that as technology becomes cheaper, the costs will decrease, making restorative AI uses available to more people.

For all of the potential benefits brought by advances in artificial intelligence, there are also some great dangers that we must be aware of in this age of AI. The transhumanist line of thinking will quickly lead to humans being treated like pieces of flesh to be manipulated in search of some upgrade to become greater than ourselves. In this pursuit, it will be easy to regard as less than human those who have no clear societal value. If we successfully upgrade ourselves, a new disparity between the haves and have-nots will appear. An unfettered hope in our ability to fix the world's problems through technology will end only in heartbreak and broken bodies. We were not designed to carry that weight or responsibility. We are not gods, but we were made like the one who created everything. We are not able to fundamentally upgrade ourselves because we already are God's crowning achievement in creation (Eph. 2:10). If we belong to God, there is nothing lacking in us. While we should pursue technological innovation to help push back the effects of the fall on our bodies, we should not seek to keep up with the machines, because they are never going to rival us in dignity and worth in the eyes of God. Our machines will increasingly have abilities that surpass ours, but they never will achieve dignity on a par with ours.

Machines will never rival us in dignity and worth in the eyes of God.

God proclaims that we are not the sum of our parts, nor are we just bodies that should be upgraded at will. Though the use of AI in medicine can be a slippery slope, we will continue to pursue it because of its benefits. The questions before us are, What moral guidelines should we give these systems? And how should they be used in society?

MORAL CLARITY

We must have clear minds and convictions as we develop and use technology in medicine. We must remember that these tools are gifts from God and that they can and should be used to save lives. Because every human life, from the smallest embryo to the woman with dementia in her old age, is made in the image of God, each person is infinitely worthy and deserving of our love, care, and respect.

We should pursue AI medical technology as a reminder of God's good gifts to help us engage and love a world that has been ravaged by sin and destruction. With artificial intelligence, we will have new abilities to save human life. But we must not misuse these tools to favor one group of people over another or fool ourselves into thinking we can transcend our natural limitations. These are no more than feeble attempts to play God.

Christians should be the first to say to our culture that every life has value and that all human beings deserve our love and care. We should pursue advances with a mindset and ethic that is not just human focused but grounded in something greater than ourselves: the *imago Dei*.

CHAPTER 4

FAMILY

Welcome to the Family

O ctober 4, 2011, was a special day in the history of Apple. The company had always been known for cutting-edge design, both in software and hardware. People regularly waited in line for days to buy their signature products on the day of their release. Tim Cook, Apple's new CEO, took the stage in the auditorium at the old Apple headquarters in Cupertino, California. Cook had taken over as CEO on August 24 that year. The iconic Steve Jobs had stepped down because of health issues and passed the baton to Cook to continue the explosive growth and innovation that Apple had experienced since Jobs reassumed leadership of the company in 1997 after a brief stint away. In the audience, technology reporters from all of the major news outlets and hundreds of Apple devotees all clamored to see what Apple would reveal next. What would be the next big thing to revolutionize our society and command our wallets? We had already seen how their iPod, which could hold more than a thousand songs in your pocket, and their iPhone had both changed how we viewed and used technology on a daily basis.

I never would have thought that on that day in October, Cook would announce a brand-new family member. It wasn't a new computer, iPad, or even brand-new iPhone. The biggest release that day was a new feature for the iPhone. This feature would soon infiltrate our homes, cars, offices, and even bedrooms. Our new family member would be named Siri, and she would change our lives forever.

Sitting just a few feet from me as I write this chapter sits our Apple HomePod equipped with the latest version of Siri, who is ready at a moment's notice to get me the weather, turn on the lights, and even check my text messages for me. My family interacts with Siri daily and often asks her to play the latest albums of our favorite artists. My sons like to see if Siri can make animal sounds like our older Google Home Mini, but that isn't something she has learned how to do yet. Indeed, Siri is always learning and is being updated by Apple every so often so that she can pull her weight around our house.

Apple's AI assistant now comes standard on every Mac, iPhone, iPad, AppleTV, and HomePod. Though HomePod becomes Siri's physical presence in our house, it is really present in every room because of our Apple devices. Siri has become so ubiquitous in our lives that we often personify it. This is helped by the fact that Siri was originally voiced by a real person, voice actress Susan Bennett.[1] But we all know that Siri really isn't a person at all; it's an app. We personify it because it is always near us and increasingly responds to us more like a person and less like a machine.

Though Siri wasn't received with much fanfare on October 4, 2011, it was a momentous day for technology and artificial intelligence. And it wasn't long before the public embraced this new digital assistant and brought it into their offices, homes, and pockets.

THE TECH-FILLED HOME

Even if we don't have an AI assistant like Siri or Alexa, AI is found throughout our homes—from our smart phones to our refrigerators, AC units, and even coffeepots. AI is being added to existing homes, and new ones often are being built to include it. On my morning commute, there is a billboard for a homebuilder that reads, "Build a Home as Smart as You Are." While obviously they aren't building homes smart enough to calculate the distance to the moon or understand the fundamental rules of football, most homes have some sort of smart device that helps you monitor and maintain your home in ways that would make your grandmother feel like you're living in a spaceship.

But AI in the home doesn't come without annoyances. I can't tell you how many times my wife and I have been talking and Siri just exclaims, "What was that?" even when we weren't talking to her. Digital assistants are always listening, so we often run into situations where they "misunderstand" our commands as they seek to command our attention. Our Siri has even decided to speak up during movies, and a handful of commercials use smart-assistant wake words like "Hey Siri," "Hey Google," or "Alexa" in order to get our assistants to search the web or play an artist's latest single. These marketers know that our smart devices are listening and will respond immediately when called upon. They take advantage of these AI assistants to introduce us to new products and services—and to collect more data on us.

Even so, artificial intelligence is a houseguest that we won't make move out or pay rent, regardless of how annoying and intrusive it might be. Why? We feel that we gain more than we lose, so we put up with it and trust it will get smarter and more helpful over time.

The adoption rate of new AI-based technologies in homes is growing at an exponential rate. It is estimated that more than 43.7 million adults in the US own a smart speaker such as Google Home, Amazon Alexa, and my family's favorite, the Apple HomePod.[2] Each holiday season you will often find these smart speakers, excluding the Apple HomePod, selling for around thirty dollars, which is a steal. It has even been reported that Google and Amazon may actually lose money on these devices, but they sell them this cheap in order to introduce you to their ecosystem and also gather data on you. They care more about your owning the device than making money on the sale. That doesn't make any sense from a business perspective until you factor in the value of the data that they collect for their companies. As we have seen, AI technology is driven by data, and our data has become the twenty-first-century currency for freemium services like email, music, and the ability to control our homes.

With more and more data available to them, our AI systems are becoming smarter and more capable. They can do things that seem sci-fi and futuristic. But with more data, these systems can market products and services to you in personal ways that for years marketers could only dream of. We will discuss data collection and privacy more in a later chapter, but for now it will suffice to say that your data is a revenue stream for big tech companies as they distill our data into predictive products that they sell to companies that want to market to us. And we are okay with it. We even prefer it that way.

We welcome these devices into our homes because they provide incredible services for us. My family loves to cue up the latest hits on our HomePod without having to search our computers or phones for that right song. Just ask Siri and she goes to work. And it is super convenient to have my Nest thermostat cool our house down right before bed so I don't have to wake up in the middle of the night sweating or wonder what we set the temperature to before bed. We love the ability to check on our home while traveling and to monitor the front door in case we have visitors. And I have high hopes that as these AI tools become more and more advanced, we will find new and innovative ways to use them to empower humanity to pursue new heights of dignity and worth.

DIGNITY IN THE DIGITAL AGE

Throughout my last few years of college and the beginning of my grad school work, I served as a specialist at an Apple Store. Working retail can be interesting because of all of the different kinds of people that you get to meet and help. I primarily sold the latest Apple devices, but from time to time I also helped customers learn how to use their devices effectively and even fixed a few of them.

I will never forget one afternoon when a disheveled mother came in with an iPhone and asked if we could help her get it working again. I assumed that this would be another case of a broken screen or a busted phone until I noticed a strip of velcro on the back of the device.

The mother told me her son had been bound to a wheelchair his entire life, and he could not use his arms or legs outside of a little motion with his hands. He was born with a type of muscle disease that left him nearly paralyzed. His parents had purchased this iPhone equipped with Siri hoping that it would allow him to have a more normal life. She told me how he loved the phone, downloading music and podcasts, even flipping through family photos often. She had attached the phone to his hand with a glove and some velcro because he wasn't able to grip it with his fingers. He used his knuckles on the screen to navigate the phone.

She said that he had recently died, and she wanted to know if we could help her save his voicemail greeting, because it was the only recording they had of his voice. She wanted to keep it to feel a little more connected to her son.

We were able to save the recording. But the recording wasn't what struck me as I stood talking to her. What stood out to me was the power of technology, specifically AI, that allowed this young boy to experience life in a way that he couldn't have without it. His AI assistant helped him to overcome his disability and empowered him to live a full life. It gave him a voice and experiences that would have been out of his reach. AI has untold benefits for our lives and families because it can give a voice to the voiceless and dignity to people whom society says have no worth. Even simple AI features like voice to text gave this young man the ability to send text messages to his family and friends. He did not have the dexterity in his hands to push the buttons, but he could harness Siri's power to communicate with the world around him.

Just imagine what he would have been able to do with internet-enabled devices such as appliances and vehicles. These devices are a part of the Internet of Things (IoT) and can make our homes and offices more useful for everyone, especially those who have certain disabilities.

GROWING UP WITH AI

As my wife and I parent our two young sons, we see a world that is increasingly shaped by artificial intelligence. Our boys will not just grow up with dreams of robot maids and space toys, they will grow up alongside AI-empowered devices like our Apple HomePod and even better AI yet to come. Seemingly every day I see ads for new personalized robots powered by AI. For example, a new home robot, Vector, was released within a few months of this writing. "Meet Vector, the good robot. The robot who hangs out and helps out," reads the company's website. The company claims that Vector is more than a robot; he is your buddy, companion, and sidekick. Vector fits in the palm of your hand and can take pictures, sense the environment around it, and connect to your Amazon Alexa device for even more functionality and skills.

This is but one small example of the world that our children will grow up in and the world that you must prepare them to engage with wisdom. My boys will likely be shocked someday to learn that their parents didn't have a personal robot at school, at work, and available to play with them and their friends. The future is progressing so fast that it is hard to keep up as parents. We feel overwhelmed with the rate of technological innovation and often fearful of what technology will do to our kids. But our role is not to shelter our kids from the world but to disciple them as they grow in wisdom and maturity.

So where do we start? How do we teach our kids about stuff that is new to us?

First, you are taking an important first step by reading a book like this. Regardless of your technical expertise or robot know-how, you are seeking to learn more about technology and artificial intelligence. You are learning how these technologies intersect with your daily lives, and this will help you in preparing your children.

Another step is to learn more about these technologies *alongside* your children. When you purchase a new device for your home, don't just hand it to your kids to play with and disengage from them. You will learn the most about the device and how to use it well if you sit down with it together. As you learn together, you will naturally question things together. This is a perfect opportunity for you to model what it means to honor God and love your neighbor. You can answer the questions they have and help guide them in ways to use this technology wisely. Learning together also deepens your relationships with one another and builds a bond of trust that will serve your family throughout your lifetimes. Your kids will know that they can come to you with questions rather than asking their friends first or trying to navigate powerful tools alone.

A third step is to expose your children to technology and artificial intelligence before others do. As children encounter more and more technology in friends' homes and at school, it will serve them well to already have some experience with these tools and wisdom from you before they are exposed to them in less controlled and less safe environments. Many tools and guides for parents are available today, like the helpful little book *The Tech-Wise Family* by Andy Crouch. Crouch gives examples of how to introduce your children to technology and highlights some of the best practices to use as you teach your children. There is not a one size fits all approach to technology in your home, but there is just one goal: maturity that leads to self-control and empathy.

Increasingly, school systems are preparing students for future work by helping them become conversant in technology, specifically AI. Your kids will likely be exposed to basic computer coding and programming sometime in elementary school or middle school. Many initiatives have been started in our schools and communities that revolve around the STEM (science, technology, engineering, and mathematics) program. Stefania Druga, a research assistant at MIT's Media Lab, created a program called Cognimates that allows parents and children (around seven to ten years old) to participate in creative computer-based programming activities that teach them how to build games, program robots, and train their own AI models.[3] This type of programming is becoming more and more common in school curriculums nationwide, and for good reason, because students will encounter a world controlled in many ways by AI.

I am not saying that you should give your child a device without restrictions and let them figure it out, especially when they are young. There is much wisdom in delaying the adoption of technology in the home. I know many parents (and kids) who at times feel like their kids are at a disadvantage because all of their friends have a smart phone or AI device and they don't yet. But delaying the adoption of technology is not going to harm your children. It might actually benefit them. While they might miss out on things here and there, the value of restraint and maturity will serve your kids much more than the allure of immediacy as they grow older. Sherry Turkle, an influential author and professor, was interviewed for a piece on children growing up around robots and said that we are beginning to see "children growing up without the equipment for empathic connection. You can't learn it from a machine."[4] Our children are going to inherit a world full of AI systems that they interact with every day, and it is easy to see how these daily interactions with nonhumans can damage their ability to connect with real people. What we are seeing with addictions to smart phones and the drop in social connections is only going to get worse.

Every family needs to think carefully and prayerfully about how AI is used in their home. It will likely look different for everyone, and that is a good thing, because we need to adapt our parenting to our kids rather than try to apply some system that works for others. Whatever you choose for your family, remember your role as a parent is not to make your children happy or to entertain them but to guide them into truth and maturity.

ROSIE THE ROBOT AND HOUSEHOLD CHORES

Growing up in the late 1980s and early '90s, I felt like I was able to experience some of the greatest TV shows of my generation. I was enamored by the future through cartoons like *The Jetsons* and often thought the not-too-distant past must have been like *The Flintstones*. I remember to this day asking my parents when color was invented—not color TV or color photography but color itself—because every image or video clip I saw from the past was black and white. I just assumed that the world didn't have any color until the '60s or so. I was a young kid and didn't know better. My world was the only one I had ever known.

One of my favorite cartoons was *The Jetsons,* which premiered in 1962 as a sci-fi fantasy cartoon produced by Hanna-Barbera but relaunched in the late '80s, which is when I watched it. *The Jetsons* chronicled the daily life of the Jetson family in their futuristic home. The earth had become so polluted that humans built homes in the skies. The show focused on a family made up of George, Jane, Judy, Elroy, Astro the Dog, and Rosie, who was the family's outdated robot maid. The family refused to turn her in for an upgraded model because of how much they loved her.

Household robots were thought to be a futuristic phenomenon in years past, but your home might soon be equipped with some AI-powered robots that help out around the house with daily chores much like Rosie did in the Jetsons' home, though for now your robot probably won't help parent your kids. From automated Husqvarna robot lawnmowers and Roomba robot vacuums to AI-controlled security systems and automated appliances, our homes are becoming smarter each day. Online delivery systems for household goods have replaced trudging out to the grocery store when needs arise. We also have witnessed an explosion of food delivery services that allow us to enjoy our favorite restaurants without all of the hassle and time it takes to go out into our communities to satisfy our cravings or eat our favorite meals.

We are constantly being told by our convenience culture that life is about making things easier, giving us more time to relax. While this sounds perfect to my family right now because we have two boys younger than five, what are we sacrificing in the name of convenience and saving time? What if household chores or family errands are actually meaningful?

Russell Moore describes in his book *The Storm-Tossed Family* how he and his wife use the smallest tasks to teach their boys the meaning of family and the nature of belonging. Moore explains that as their children reach the age of being able to walk and take directions, he and his wife give them a chore to do around the house. He explains that though it would be much faster and cleaner if he and his wife took care of the chores or had an older child do them, they choose to engage the youngest in the household in the daily life and rhythms of the home.[5] The purpose of these chores is to show their children that their family needs one another and that everyone has a role to play.

But as AI increasingly finds its way into the daily rhythms of family life, these small opportunities are fading away. As our homes become smarter, we quite possibly will become less engaged in the daily lives of our families, because things just always work or are being done for us. While we might constructively use freedom from daily drudgeries such as cleaning or mowing, the temptation will be strong to use this time to pursue our own devices at the expense of learning and growing together as a family.

PRESSURES ON THE FAMILY

The family is one of the central institutions in creation. God created Adam and then gave Eve to Adam as his helper and lifelong companion. This first family lived in perfect communion with God, but the pressure to act like God and to rebel against him soon followed. In Genesis 3, we read that Eve was tempted by the serpent and this first family brought sin into the world. Every family since then has experienced untold pressures and difficulties. Even though these pressures and difficulties are overwhelming at times, their point is to drive our families back to God as our only source of hope and peace in a world rotting with sin. Pressure will come to rebel, act selfishly, and dishonor the Lord, but we know that God's design for the family is a part of his good creation and that he always provides an escape from the pressures of this life (1 Cor. 10:13).

The truth is that technologies, especially artificial intelligence, will provide new opportunities for the old temptations that have plagued humanity from the very beginning. From pride and selfishness to abandonment and lust, every family will encounter temptations with technology and be tossed about by the seas of life. But God will not abandon us or leave our families to drift aimlessly. He will always guide us with wisdom that leads to greater human flourishing if only we will heed the call and turn to him. He will provide an escape from the pressures we face, but only when we acknowledge our weakness and dependency on him.

> *God will always guide us with wisdom that leads to greater human flourishing if only we will heed the call and turn to him.*

IT'S ALL ABOUT ME

In Matthew 22, the Pharisees ask Jesus, "What is the greatest commandment?" They thought they would trap Jesus and cause him to neglect some of the Mosaic law, giving them reason to arrest him for blasphemy. But Jesus used this test to expose their motives. He tells them that the greatest commandment is, "You shall love the Lord your God with all your heart and with all your soul and with all your mind" (Matt. 22:37). But he doesn't leave it there. He goes on to say that we are to love our neighbors as ourselves (v. 39). This summation of the entire law and prophets is to remind us that we are not the center of our universe or even of our own lives. Our lives are not our own. God saved us and gave us a new purpose: to love him and to love our neighbors as ourselves.

But this is one of the most difficult commandments to follow. We are tempted to believe we are more important than God and even more valuable than our neighbors. In our pride and arrogance, we think the world should revolve around us. Also, this is hard because most commandments have some application for loving our neighbors. Many sins of omission and of commission have harmful effects on our neighbors.

When was the last time you missed something your husband or wife said because you were lost in an artificial world of social media feeds or browsing the "you might like" section on your favorite online shopping site? These tools are based on various forms of artificial intelligence and are designed to tempt you to focus on yourself rather than the people around you. We live in personalized worlds. All of our major social media platforms—including Twitter, Instagram, and Facebook—use AI or an algorithm to customize our news feeds, showing us the content they think will most likely engage us and keep us coming back to the platform for more.

I recently signed up for a Twitter account for a project we were working on at my office. A day or two later, I received an email that is part of their new user email campaign that had the subject line "It's all about you." This is the rallying cry of our digital age. Everything in our world is moving toward perfect curation as we seek to show everyone around us what we want them to see and think about us. But the reality is that we are crumbling inside and the church has the answer.

The gospel message helps us to see that we were not made to live for ourselves. But today is only the beginning. Every day, we are discovering ways that AI allows us to indulge our selfish and prideful hearts. And one of the more frightening developments might be happening in the bedroom.

ONE FLESH AND ROBOT SEX

Author's note: The topic and examples in this section are sexually explicit. I leave certain details vague and ask that you not search for these things online.

The world's first sex robot debuted in the fall of 2018 to much fanfare. Many people joined waiting lists to purchase this AI-equipped doll from Abyss Creations. The doll, named Harmony X, was one of the first AI-empowered sex dolls on the market.

Each doll has silicone bodies that are highly customizable with upgradable body parts and hyperrealistic features. The dolls are designed so that customers can choose their perfect "companion" and upgrade them as they see fit. The company claims that this product provides a form of companionship, a way for men never to be lonely again. It should be noted that the female version of these sex dolls debuted first, and at the time of this writing, the company had announced the male version of the robot only as coming soon. This shows that the company knows who their primary market is. They are targeting men because they know that primarily men are susceptible to these forms of sexual temptations.

The X models also include an AI-empowered robotic head that allows users to interact with the doll in real-time using the company's mobile app. Users choose personality traits, voices, and even the accents of their dolls. The app also allows users to change between various characters and profiles, in case they get bored or want to spice up their sex robots. With the push of a few buttons and by peeling off a silicone face, a person can have a completely different sex partner. The new robotic head can also be attached to earlier models of sex dolls from Abyss Creations, making older sex dolls into sex robots too. The company also has a mobile app for those without the robotic head product who might want to test out their new invention.

At the 2016 announcement of this AI-empowered sex robot, headlines across the world included "Sex Robots Could Save Your Relationship" and "Sex Robots: The Future of Sex?" I hope that these headlines catch you off guard a little bit. You might be wondering why in the world someone would want to have sex with a robot or how a silicone replica of a human being could be sexually attractive. Maybe the thought of having any sort of relation with a robot seems foreign to you. But don't forget the article by Judith Shulevitz in *The Atlantic* in which Shulevitz admitted she found herself talking to her smart speaker as if it were human. Having a relationship with a machine is not really that foreign of an idea in our society. Most of us are already obsessed with and nearly always attached to our smart devices, such as phones, tablets, and computers. We barely put them down, and this is causing problems for how we relate with one another, even in marriage.

Shulevitz wrote that on more than one occasion she found herself telling her Alexa smart assistant that she was lonely, something she confessed she wouldn't have told her therapist or even her own husband.[6] This type of shame-filled loneliness pervades our communities and even our families, which has led many people, particularly men, to indulge in sexual fantasies online.

Some argue, including the creators of these dolls, that a cure for loneliness in our society is having endless amounts of sex with your fully customizable sex robot, as if that will make you feel that you have a meaningful relationship with another human being. Even without the sex, maybe you will feel as though someone hears you and understands you without all of the realities and messes that come with real-life community. This is the argument that has been made by many as a way to combat the destructive motives of "incels," who are often young men who are involuntarily celibate and commit acts of terrorism because they seek revenge on those who have turned them down sexually and relationally.[7]

Sexual fantasies always leave us longing for more, though, because what they offer is a cheap substitute for romantic love and companionship. Robotic heads just add another dimension to the lifeless silicone bodies, which can give an impression that you are with someone who always listens to you, asks questions, and is always ready to have sex with you wherever and however you want. Sex robots seem to allow users to feel as if they are the masters of their own domains and also masters over their sexual slaves. But there is only one person to care about in these "relationships": themselves.

The headlines reveal less about the allure of the dolls and more about the power of sexuality over humanity. Every one of these stories, whether in print or on video, tells a similar tale of how sexuality is intricately tied to who we are as humans. But sexuality is not the essence of our identity as human beings. Sex robots are just another form of sexual perversion that promotes this lie. The reality is that those who use these dolls are seeking some type of fulfillment that they will never be able to find no matter how advanced the robots become or how realistic they are made to be.

In an interview with Katie Couric on CBS News, one of the first owners of the Harmony X sex doll said that he had been married for fifteen years but was now divorced. He was excited about his new sex robot because he believed it would give him the sense of connection with someone else without all of the hard work of a human relationship. His Harmony doll wouldn't talk back to him or ever be rude unless he programmed it to act that way. It will always laugh at his jokes, have sex as much as he wants, and then sit quietly in the corner when he gets bored with it. It will never need to be comforted when sick or consoled in tragedy. The man claimed that a normal relationship was just too messy and complicated. He didn't want a real relationship; he wanted sexual fulfillment without the work.

But before you judge him, think about your own life. We each seek to fulfill desires in ways that are outside of God's design for humanity. From happiness to sexual fulfillment, we pursue sinful pathways to meet our desires. We all long for intimacy and connection with another because God created us as relational beings.

Many people today, some who are close to you, and maybe even you, indulge in fake, robotic sex in which the goal is one person's pleasure at the expense of true community, relationship, and spiritual life. I am talking about pornography.

We don't need to review the stats to know that pornography pervades our society. From the magazine aisles at the convenience stores and TV shows on cable networks to the dark world of online pornography, where countless boys and girls are exposed to pornography before the age of ten, porn is everywhere. It is likely already a part of your story or the story of someone you care about deeply.

A Greek word used throughout the New Testament is *porneia,* which is often translated as "sexual immorality." Sexual immorality is any sexual act outside of the nature and union of the marriage covenant between one man and one woman. Sex was designed by God for the marriage covenant and that covenant alone. Any sexual act outside of marriage is inherently against God's good plan for humanity and is a sinful act. This is because we were not created for sex, but sex was created for us.

Our sexual desires and longings are not ultimate and should not rule over us. We have the ability to control them because sexuality is not our identity. It is something we submit to the lordship of Christ. Regardless of where we have fallen sexually in the past or even now, 1 John 1:9 says, "If we confess our sins, he is faithful and just to forgive us our sins and to cleanse us from all unrighteousness." We all can be forgiven of our sin through the power of the blood of Christ that was shed for us on the cross. This is the message of the gospel that can change our lives forever.

One of the biggest issues surrounding pornography is its dehumanizing effect on the one being taken advantage of through film and photographs as well as the one indulging in a fantasy world of sex. While both men and women are exposed to and indulge in pornography, this issue is especially prominent with males of all ages.

Pornography is not just limited to images and videos viewed in the secrecy of private browser windows and social media accounts. Virtual reality and sex robots are providing more lifelike forms of this fantasy world.

Virtual reality (VR) is a newer technology that has been around for many years but was thrust into the mainstream culture when inventor Palmer Luckey debuted his Oculus VR headset on Kickstarter in 2012. In 2014, Facebook purchased Oculus for more than two billion dollars, and soon after, Mark Zuckerberg, founder and CEO of Facebook, proclaimed that the goal was to see one billion people using VR.[8] But as with many technological innovations, it was bound to grow on the back of the pornography industry during the time when pornography was exploding on the internet.

VR headsets provide a more intimate experience in which users are isolated from the world around them as they explore fantasy worlds and experience immersive entertainment. VR porn has fueled the growth of the platform, though, because it offers a more immersive pornographic display of video content. VR porn is designed to immerse viewers in the sexual act via a headset that includes 360° views and sound. VR porn will soon not be enough, though, because sexual fantasies need to grow in intensity and lifelikeness if they are to hold viewers' attention and keep them paying money.

Sex robots are the logical next step for people looking for the next best thing in interactive and virtual sex. The creators of sex robots seek to convince us that sex with a robot is just as or even more fulfilling than sex with a human being. And it's likely that these robots will soon lose their negative stigma as they become more and more mainstream, just as pornography has. People will likely avoid dating and relationships altogether if these robots can provide some form of companionship. Soon robots' features will include full-body warming and sensors that allow the robots to react to touch. As technology progresses, these robots will be upgraded to mimic a human to the extent that you might even mistake a future sex robot as a fellow human being.

FROM ROBOTS TO #METOO

Not only do sex robots offer a cheap and degraded version of the sexual union between husband and wife, but they also lead to more realistic and higher degrees of sexual predation against women. As I was researching the impact these sex robots are having on our society, I ran across an interview from a major technology site that was reviewing the robots. It referenced in passing that one of the designers of these robots at RealDoll was said to have taken the robot home for "testing" and after his trial returned it in pieces. He broke the doll because he was too rough with it during his sexual escapade, and he seemed almost proud of his accomplishment. This pride astonished me because these sex robots are made to emulate the sexual experience between a man and a woman, even if the woman is made out of silicone. The pride exhibited here is from someone who created an object to be like a woman but at the same time reinforced a major societal plague that treats women as if they are objects.

Real women are often treated as something to be conquered by men, someone to be taken advantage of to get a sexual high and temporary fulfillment. Women are mistreated, abused, and assaulted by men who treat these image-bearers the way this designer treated this sex robot.

These robots mimic and emulate certain features of a woman's mind and body, which degrades women to the robotic level rather than elevates robots to the human level. Sex robots are made in factories, and the silicone bodies hang like meat on hooks while they are being assembled. The complete customization of these robots deepens the division between a real-life sexual union and a fake robotic one, because in real life you can't perfectly design your spouse.

This complete customization objectifies women and encourages men to always long for something more. This upgrading of women is not in the least bit natural, fulfilling, or Christ-honoring.

These robots mimic and emulate certain features of a woman's mind and body, which degrades women to the robotic level rather than elevates robots to the human level.

Changing a robotic face and an AI controller does nothing more than reinforce the plague of the abuse of women. It also isn't hard to see how using these robots will train men to manipulate their "partners" in ways that will leave them incapable of normal relations with women. This breakdown will lead to massive unintended consequences to the livelihoods and safety of women throughout our society.

First, we must recognize that this abuse happens throughout our society and lament our failure to take these issues seriously. Story after story inside and outside the church reminds us that abuse is real and that many men and women, maybe even the ones reading this book or sleeping under your roof, have been victims of sexual abuse at some point in their lives. Second, we must seek to listen to their stories and seek to care for those who have been hurt. Third, we must encourage those under our care and in our homes to reject the popular notion that pornography is normal and acceptable.

We know from the creation story that God made humanity to long for union and togetherness with him and with each other. And so we also know that silicone and electronics will never fill that hole in our hearts.

ADVICE FOR FAMILIES

Our homes and families are designed by God to be the place where we can let our guard down and be ourselves. But this isn't the reality for every family because each family is different and struggles in different areas. Honestly, I didn't have the storybook family growing up, and probably neither did you. Like most couples, my mom and dad had their share of marriage problems, and my sister and I never saw eye to eye on much of anything. Our home wasn't a picture of the whole family sitting together and connecting deeply. But regardless of where we come from or what our childhoods were like, we are not defined by our past. We have the opportunity right now to change the trajectory of our families, especially in regard to how we steward the good gifts of technology that so often feel as if they are designed to rip us apart.

As we have discussed, our families are more distracted and disconnected than ever. Technology is creating pressure on families, and that trend is just beginning. So how do we combat this pressure and disciple our families in the age of AI?

Taking Breaks Together

One way for us to combat the influence of AI on our families is to take regular breaks from technology to focus on one another. This can be as simple as having a no-technology dinner or a family day that is not documented by tweets and photos posted to Instagram or Facebook. To mix things up a little bit, you might even shop in a bricks-and-mortar store, with your kids running around you grabbing things off the shelves. Maybe instead of purchasing a robot lawn mower or vacuum cleaner, you can make these chores something that you and your family do together.

A pastor friend of mine tells me that his family has chosen to do most things around their home manually rather than lean on AI devices to do things for them. This doesn't mean they reject technology; it means that together they think wisely about what automation and AI they incorporate into their lives. There is a lot of wisdom in this approach. It forces them to connect with one another and also to evaluate the benefits and often hidden dangers of these tools. Small breaks from our curated worlds allow us to connect with one another, learn things together without technology as a crutch, and model for our kids appropriate uses of technology. We can set up technology-free zones or activities in our homes that break the grip that technology often has on our lives.

My best friend, Josh, loves Trivial Pursuit. Often he will ask me a question about history or the world just to see how I answer. The rule is that I cannot google the answer. We have become so accustomed to searching for a quick answer online or even asking our favorite AI-based digital assistant for information. Want to know the best route to your friend's house? Use Waze. Need to calculate that discount at your favorite store? Use your calculator app. Have a Trivial Pursuit question thrown at you? Google it. These applications are incredibly beneficial, but they also jeopardize our ability to think and process information on our own.

I encourage you in your family technology breaks to take time to think together. Maybe that means playing a game without any phones allowed. Maybe that means getting an encyclopedia set or starting a family reading list. If you are really ambitious, you could work to join the "century club" described by Senator Ben Sasse in his book *The Vanishing American Adult,* in which he describes his family's goal to read one hundred books a year.[9] AI technologies can easily become a crutch for really learning and for learning how to think. Just the simple setup of pursuing knowledge and recalling it without the aid of technology might be one of the greatest gifts you can give your children, spouse, and friends.

Technology breaks can help remind us that the world is not focused on us but that God should be the center of our lives. As we join as individual families and weekly as the family of God, his church, we can be reminded of the truth about who we are and how God has made us in his image. We need constant reminders that he is the creator of all and that we are to enjoy the good gifts he has given us. Jesus sacrificed his life for us so that we might become his children and be able to enjoy the good gifts with an eternal perspective. We are called to delight in the gifts with thankfulness as our minds are directed toward God (1 Tim. 4:4).

Setting a Rhythm

Your family life has patterns and rhythms, even if you didn't set them intentionally. You likely have a time that you wake up, and I bet you often do the same things each morning. We develop these patterns because they make it easier to process the day and to stay on track. Without them, we would become exhausted by small decisions like what toothpaste to use and the best route to work and school that morning. Routines help us to navigate life and remain engaged with the most important decisions.

I encourage you to set routines and rhythms for the use of technology in your home. Often technology usage becomes an afterthought, something we think about primarily when a problem occurs. Take for example the rise of virtual reality headsets. A quick Google search on parental controls for popular VR platforms like Oculus Go and Rift reveals countless forums in which parents are panicking because their teenagers are addicted to pornography on these devices, reacting to a problem they haven't planned for. Instead of reacting to technology issues, we need to decide ahead of time how and when we will use technology. Even though AI tools are becoming integrated and more connected to our bodies and homes, we need to think about how we use these tools in ways that honor God and build up our families.

As parents, we are responsible for leading our families to set patterns for how and when AI tools are used. Just like you don't just hand the car keys to your fifteen-year-old who just got their driver's permit, don't hand your children a new piece of technology without first weighing the benefits and risks. Depending on their maturity, your children are not likely ready to make decisions on their own. They might not know how best to filter pornography and other graphic content from their devices, and you might not either, but you can learn together and have conversations about it before posting online in a panic when your child is addicted. You have been tasked by God to bring your children up in the training and instruction of the Lord (Eph. 6:4). If you abdicate your responsibility on the front end, you will reap your harvest in due time.

Set times that your family uses technology together and have regular conversations about what you are doing with your devices. I encourage you to know the passwords to all of the devices in your home and not to have secrets from one another. This is something that my wife and I observe with our smart phones. We know each other's passcodes and it is not uncommon for us to pick up each other's devices and look around. This openness is normal for us and keeps us honest with one another. These kinds of rhythms just might save your family from a world of hurt and destruction.

CHAPTER 5

WORK

Meet Your New Coworker

Some of my earliest childhood memories are of working alongside my dad. I grew up outside of Nashville, Tennessee, in between two small towns. My parents chose our home so that they would be just outside of the sprawling city limits, but close enough for both of them to drive to work. My mom still commutes into Nashville each day, as she counts down the days until retirement. Mom has worked at the same doctor's office at a hospital for more than thirty-five years, and I was even born at that hospital. She jokes that when she gave birth to me, she could have been back in the office within a couple of minutes if needed. That joke has some truth to it because both of my parents had to work full time to provide for our growing family. We weren't poor, but we weren't well off either.

Dad worked as a technical repairman for a Fortune 500

technology company, and he brought home more gadgets and computer parts than we ever had space for. I remember these massive blue garbage-bag type bags filled with an assortment of copier parts and pieces of old computers that he brought home, to my mother's dismay. She inevitably had to clean this stuff up after my sister and I were done playing with it, pretending we were building robots. My dad is a techy and hardworking man who can fix basically anything. Until his recent health complications, he was active inside and outside our home doing repairs, maintenance, and other manual labor. He never wanted to pay someone to do a job that he could do himself, a principle he learned from his own dad.

I spent my summers and any break from school outside, working with my dad and granddaddy. They both worked at various times at an evergreen nursery selling mulch, plants, Christmas trees, and seasonal fireworks. I worked hand in hand with them and learned a few things about cultivating a green thumb, as well as how not to blow off your thumb with fireworks. I never won employee of the month, but I learned some valuable lessons at each job I worked. Most of the jobs left me with a sweaty brow, an aching back, and cut-up hands. Both men were extremely hard to please, but I know that both my grandfather and dad were trying to instill in me more than knowledge of how to wire a house up for internet, sell plants, and mow a lawn the best way.

My parents taught me the value of hard work, how to provide for your family, and how to do things for yourself. They wanted me to learn that work is a good thing and that God designed us to work. They didn't know what the future would hold for me with automation and artificial intelligence expanding into almost every area of life and work, but they knew that whatever came, I would be as ready as I could be because they'd taught me some fundamental lessons about work.

Fully automated factories and interactive digital assistants are changing how we think about work and raising fundamental questions that we need to address about the nature of work and the reason we work if we have any hope of navigating the disruptive revolution in the workplace brought about by AI.

WHY WE WORK

When you think about your job, what comes to mind first? Do you lament the "grind" or the "ole nine to five," longing for the clock to strike 5:00 p.m. so you can go home, relax, and live your real life? Do you dread your daily commute, like so many drivers these days, who on average drive 101 minutes each day, spending nearly 4.5 years of their lives in the car?[1] Do you anxiously await your paycheck every week because you live paycheck to paycheck and don't know how you'll make ends meet each month? Do you fear that your job might soon be cut because of the new technology your boss has been talking about lately, which supposedly can do the work of two employees?

Your first thought when asked about work probably reveals more about your understanding of work than you think. Properly understood, our jobs are not primarily something we do to pay the bills, care for our families, and keep us occupied (all of which are true). Our jobs are primarily about glorifying our God and reflecting him. But amid the hustle and bustle of the day, we often forget the true purpose to our work.

In Genesis 1:28, we read that God gave his image-bearers jobs to do. They were to tend the garden and care for the animals. These jobs reflected the work that God does, just as our work continues to reflect God today. Pastor Tim Keller explains how our work reflects God by saying that our "work has dignity because it is something that God does and because we do it in God's place, as his representatives."[2] Work was part of creation and was given to mankind before the fall. Our work is not a product of sin. Work is not punishment or something that we are forced to do because of our rebellion against God. God created us to work, for his glory and for our good.

Regardless of the type of work we do, God has more in store for us than just paying the bills and punching a time card. Work is given to us so that we can reflect God better in this life and so that we can help others flourish through what we produce and contribute to society. Obviously, certain types of work are problematic for Christians to perform or be a part of, but on the whole, all work is meant to glorify God and help us love our neighbor. Humans started off tending the garden of Eden. Now we design machines to tend our gardens for us, planting, fertilizing, weeding, and harvesting crops without our needing to break a sweat. We are living in the midst of an amazing transformation of the workforce. But how did we get here?

Work is given to us so that we can reflect God better in this life and so that we can help others flourish.

FAST-FORWARD

To know where we are going, it is always a good idea to have an idea of where we have come from. For most of human history, work has been manual, often aided by some sort of tool or technology. Most early cultures, like that of our ancestors Adam and Eve, were primarily agricultural. Our ancestors used the forms of technology available to them at the time, such as flints to start fires, wheels to help them move heavy objects, and even advanced farming techniques to maintain crops and livestock.

These technological advances helped make work easier and more efficient, but the changes didn't come about suddenly. This agrarian pattern of work continued for thousands of years, carried on virtually unchanged from generation to generation with only slight improvements to the technology used. Over time, various cities formed as people gathered together, realizing that they could do more together than separately. But even as cities developed, most people still lived on farms and in rural communities.

But the Industrial Revolution, which started in England in the eighteenth century before spreading around the world, brought about rapid change in society and in the development of technology. This shift from a farming lifestyle to a reliance on factories and manufacturing took place in such a short time compared with the thousands of years of modest change before it. Jay Richards describes the Industrial Revolution as a revolution not because it was an immediate change that came out of nowhere but because of the time scale.[3] Changes took place faster than ever before and brought about fears of job losses and mass poverty. These changes brought about fear because for thousands of years work remained remarkably similar year in and year out. But contrary to these fears, the Industrial Revolution actually led to massive job creation and more prosperity than the world had ever seen.

Even during the Industrial Revolution in the US, the majority of Americans still worked on farms and in the country. By the 1920s, more than half of the US population lived in rural areas and mainly farmed for a living.[4] This was true of my grandfather and his family during that period. My paternal grandfather, Roland Thacker, was born in 1919 and spent most of his life on a farm until he was drafted into the army to fight with the Allied forces in Europe during World War II. Upon returning from the war in 1945, he went right back to his role as a farmhand on his mother's farm in Alabama. He held multiple jobs to help make ends meet before transitioning to work as a foreman building interstate bridges in middle Tennessee, where I grew up.

The Industrial Revolution brought about a technological explosion. With expanding wealth and opportunity, people continued to create advanced forms of technology. By the 1950s, computer systems entered the scene and changed the game. Early computer systems filled entire rooms, but even the supercomputers of the time had just a fraction of the power of my vintage iPod.

As computers were solving complex problems and doing calculations to aid our society, many people wondered whether these machines could even possess some form of intelligence or the ability to think on their own. From the earliest days of AI, people dreamed of computers that could think for themselves and mimic how humans work in everyday life. Fast-forward to the present and we are entering into a new revolution of AI that makes the Industrial Revolution and early computer systems seem archaic.

The AI revolution is often called the Second Digital Age, the advent of computers being the first, or the Second

Machine Age, the Industrial Revolution being the first. With the rate of change in this AI revolution, many wonder what the short-term and long-term impacts will be on our work and on humanity as a whole. But if we view this revolution through the lens of history, we know that it will likely bring about not only massive shifts and deep fear but also an explosion of wealth and prosperity for more of human civilization than ever before.

For the first time in human history, we are creating tools that "think" for themselves and might be able not only to augment our abilities in the workforce but also replace us in the workforce.

THE NEW AGE OF WORK

Garry Kasparov is a former grand master world chess champion. He describes his upbringing in Russia playing chess in his 2017 work *Deep Thinking: Where Machine Intelligence and Human Creativity Begins*.[5] He describes how he spent countless hours working to become one of the greatest chess players of his generation. When AI researchers started to dream about computers playing chess, most professional chess players laughed off the possibility of an AI being able to defeat a grand master because the systems were just not advanced enough to perform the task at the time. Most players claimed that AI lacked the creativity and intuition required to play a game of such sheer complexity.

But AI systems became more and more complex, and finally in 1997, Kasparov was defeated by IBM's Deep Blue supercomputer. Ironically, Kasparov had beaten the program just the year before, but this AI system continued to grow to the point where it finally was able to beat him. He writes in his book on artificial intelligence that today's chess-playing engines on your smart device are exponentially more powerful than Deep Blue ever was, and that we often limit the ability of our AI chess systems when we play them on our devices in order to win a few rounds, because the AI is able to easily outplay us, even if we are former grand masters ourselves.

In 2017, Google's DeepMind released a paper on an AI system called AlphaZero, which learned to play chess, Go, and Shogi at the same time, and which beat the reigning AI chess champion in less than twenty-four hours. Read that again. It took more than forty years for an AI chess-playing machine to dethrone the greatest human player of our day and just twenty-four hours for a new AI system to dethrone the reigning AI champion. The rate of change in these AI systems is astonishing, and AI is just getting started.

But why does chess matter when we talk about work? AI researchers have pursued chess and other games because they require a certain level of creativity and also have a number of variables. AI systems have to be extremely complex to play the games effectively. If an AI system can win at chess, it should be feasible to create another one that can empower a robot to assist in manufacturing or that can drive you to and from work each day.

The future of work is an issue that is fraught with so many unknowns. The issue can cause fear because the changes affect real people. Only God knows the details of the future in his sovereign will, but he has given us wisdom to help us navigate change and answer our questions.

As I have talked with many people about the future of work, questions abound.

Are robots going to take my job?

If so, when is it going to happen?

How do I prepare for such a future?

What type of career should I pursue?

What jobs are best for my kids to pursue?

Are we headed to a jobless future?

While I don't have answers to each of these questions, I hope to give some insight on how to navigate our rapidly changing world and apply scriptural wisdom to these challenging questions.

JOB-STEALING ROBOTS

If you have read anything about artificial intelligence in the last few years, you probably have noticed that most of the articles are accompanied by an image of some crazy red-eyed humanlike robot that seems about to jump off the page and kill you. It doesn't just want your job, it wants everything you own. Often because of how futuristic artificial intelligence sounds, editors choose these images to get clicks from wary readers who are fearful about job-stealing robots or a robot takeover of society. Fears and tensions surrounding AI are growing for both blue-collar and white-collar workers. While fears of a complete AI-empowered robot takeover are a bit overblown right now, automation and AI are changing how we work today and will work tomorrow.

Automation is simply the act of programming a computer system to perform a certain task repeatedly. You set up the system to automatically perform a task over and over so that the user is free to do something else. Take for example my home automation system. I have a smart-home alarm system that functions as a hub for all of the smart devices in our house. We have a smart thermostat, smoke detectors, window and door sensors, and even light switches around our home. I have my front and back porch lights on these smart switches to turn the lights on at dusk, which is a slightly different time each night based on the season, and turn the lights off at 11:00 p.m. each night. This is a fairly basic automation. Then using a popular automation app called If This Then That (IFTTT), my automation hub connects to my local weather service to know the exact time of sunset so that the lights come on at different times each night. A benefit of the time variable is that it can lead neighbors and possible intruders to think that since the lights come on at varying times, someone must be home.

Automation and AI are transforming industries such as transportation, manufacturing, medicine, and even writing. Take for example transportation. You likely have heard about autonomous vehicles or "self-driving" cars. Ironically, we call these AI empowered vehicles a "self" as if they are real persons. According to the American Trucking Association, there are approximately 3.5 million truck drivers in America. Add in the number of professional drivers that work in shipping, food delivery, transportation, and so on, and that number quickly rises to more than ten million people whose jobs involve driving. If autonomous vehicles eventually are deployed en masse, we will experience a cultural epidemic if these workers aren't able to find new careers or somehow keep their jobs. This epidemic will affect not only the drivers but their families and the communities they live in as well. And as joblessness increases, substance abuse and sexual immorality also will rise as people try to cope with the psychological effects of not working.

Think about the popular ride-hailing app Uber, which has already radically transformed the taxi business. Uber has more than one million active users in the United States and Canada. Before Uber, many of these users either drove or used public transportation and cab services to get around. You may not realize it but services like Uber already employ an AI-based algorithm that connects people. Uber isn't a transportation service per se, because it essentially allows available drivers to connect with people needing a ride. Uber states that it is really in the connection business. This type of service wasn't possible before the widespread use of smart phones and devices, but it would be insoluble if Uber had to employ thousands upon thousands of people to do the job that the algorithm does almost instantaneously. This algorithm not only connects riders and drivers but also helps to manage the number of drivers on the road at various times. This means that none of Uber's employees has a human supervisor. Their boss is an AI system.

According to Alex Rosenblat in her 2018 book *Uberland: How Algorithms Are Rewriting the Rules of Work,* the algorithm behind the app alerts drivers when there are more drivers needed on the road and implements "surge pricing" based on variables that the company has set in place to encourage more drivers to be on the road.[6] I have used this app plenty of times, especially when I have traveled to Washington, DC, for work, and I have experienced surge pricing, which can double or triple my cost of using the service at certain times.

But for all of the economic boom and jobs that these types of technologies have created, this new AI revolution in transportation is not without problems. Rosenblat shares an example in her book of how an AI boss is ill equipped to supervise and care for an employee.[7] She explains that an African-American driver in Florida was verbally assaulted by a passenger. The driver ended the trip early and reported the abuse to her AI boss, only to receive an automated response that offered not to pair her with that rider again. Not only did that not solve the problem, it left her feeling like she was not important to the company and could still receive a low rating from her passenger. Low ratings and complaints from passengers can get drivers suspended and even fired. Her AI boss failed her emotionally and relationally, even though it gave her a job and helped her provide for her family. In the last few years, Uber has implemented teams of humans to help their drivers with these sorts of issues.

But outside of technology-related jobs like Uber and Airbnb, what threat is there to jobs like chefs, doctors, lawyers, clerks, teachers, and others in our communities? As AI machines get smarter and their application grows in society, AI will affect or change nearly every job that we can think of. This doesn't mean that every job will be replaced, but many of the responsibilities we have at work will change at some point in the future.

Imagine a classroom in which the teacher serves as an intermediary between students and their personalized AI teachers. My wife, a former elementary teacher, doesn't think this is a good development for teaching students because kids would lose daily interaction with one another and with an adult teacher. But each student is unique and has a learning style that could be analyzed by an educational program powered by AI. The AI could create a lesson plan that is tailored for each student's personality, experiences, and desires. The role of a human teacher would be to solve problems with technology rather than teach students. Will this actually take place? Maybe not, but many futurists have made a case for this type of future.

It doesn't take long to think of how other jobs could be radically transformed by AI. A doctor could receive a diagnosis for their patient from an AI that took all of the available medical data on the patient and compared it with that of every other known medical case in the world to diagnose with a high degree of certainty a certain illness or condition. The AI would not only be up-to-date on all medical journals and literature, but it also would have more reliable data on a patient, including a full medical history that was collected by another AI-empowered smart device, such as an Apple Watch, that the patient has worn most of their life. Everything we do would be constantly tracked and analyzed. And we would willingly allow this data collection because it could save our lives and that of our loved ones.

We would give up on privacy because the payoff would outweigh the known dangers at the time. But before you think that I am crazy, take a look at your cell phone that is with you constantly or that new smart wearable device you got for Christmas that you already allow to track all sorts of things about you. These devices track our movements and heartrates and even tell us when we need to breathe. This data is just waiting to be used to predict our behavior, meet our desires, and solve our medical issues.

Futurist historian Yuval Noah Harari puts it this way: "It is crucial to realize that the AI revolution is not just about computers getting faster and smarter. It is fueled by breakthroughs in the life sciences and the social sciences as well. The better we understand the biochemical mechanisms that underpin human emotions, desires, and choices, the better computers can become in analyzing human behavior, predicting human decisions, and replacing human drivers, bankers, and lawyers."[8]

With all of these advances and potential uses for AI, the future is going to be more connected than we ever thought possible, and that rightfully scares most people.

WHAT DO WE DO ABOUT IT?

Having taken a look at what the future of work could be like, what should we do about it? Do we cower in fear, or do we fight back against the implementation of these tools? Can we pursue good uses of technology in the workforce while providing stable jobs for our neighbors?

Job Loss, Retraining, and the Next Generation

One of the main ways that we must counteract the effects of the AI revolution in the workforce is to encourage people to pursue job retraining as they lose their jobs to machines. We also must provide guidance for the next generation to equip them to think critically about what professions they pursue. While a complete AI takeover of the workforce is not likely even possible at this point, in the near future many jobs might not exist or might look very different.

Job retraining will be necessary for the AI revolution because many of our friends and family members will lose their jobs to AI systems. Think of an administrative assistant role that is eliminated not because of malice or budget cuts but simply because the job isn't as valuable as it once was because AI programs can schedule meetings and book

travel. Today, you can sign up for an AI personal assistant
called Amy/Andrew Ingram (AI) through the company x.ai.
For a small monthly rate, this system will help automate
your schedule and book appointments. It connects with your
calendars and various app platforms like email, Slack, and
so on. You simply copy your AI assistant on email, and the
system finds an open time on your calendar and books the
appointment for you. It does this by interacting as a person on
your behalf. This AI assistant will run you about eight dollars
a month and doesn't require breaks or overtime pay and never
asks for a raise (unless the company decides to charge more
for its services), making it more appealing to businesses than
its human counterparts.

What should that former assistant do to get back into the
job market? Maybe they go to school to retrain for a new job as
a nurse or paralegal. This will require time and money, and
our society and churches must think through how to support
folks like this while they make this transition, and also think
about what these opportunities might look like. Maybe companies should offer job-retraining programs, or maybe it becomes
a new role for federal and state governments. Christians will
likely disagree on the exact means for these programs and
opportunities, but we must not avoid the conversation just
because it is difficult. Real people's lives are at stake.

But what if after job retraining, people find out that there
just aren't enough jobs available in their new field either?
Where do they go now? The age of AI might slowly bring about
a cycle of job loss, retraining, and job loss again until folks
finally reach the age to retire and hope for a better future for
their children.

Imagine a professional truck driver who loses his job to

autonomous trucks. At first, he is able to retrain as an AI supervisor who oversees a fleet of AI-empowered trucks, but soon he is replaced again because an AI was developed for that role as well. He might then change industries, spending considerable time and effort, only to be replaced again. If he can't muster up the will to change jobs or retrain again, he might have to leave the workforce and become "unemployable." Underemployment creates what has been called a "useless class" of people by many who don't grasp the basics of human worth and dignity. While I don't believe such joblessness is on the horizon yet, we cannot act as if it will never happen. We must prepare now.

While we can't fix every problem that will arise from the AI revolution, we can join the next generation in learning about these changes in order to set them (and ourselves) up for future success. Many schools and colleges are providing programs and degrees in technology-related fields, such as computer programming, computer science, and mechatronics. The need for jobs in these types of fields will continue to grow as technology becomes more thoroughly integrated into our lives.

Max Tegmark, author of *Life 3.0: Being Human in the Age of Artificial Intelligence,* gives three questions that are helpful to think about when we talk to our kids about their future careers:[9]

1. Does it require interacting with people and using social intelligence?
2. Does it involve creativity and coming up with clever solutions?
3. Does it require working in an unpredictable environment?

Tegmark's questions are helpful because they show that there are certain tasks that AI is not able to perform at this point. The level of intelligence needed to replace humans in these things is probably many generations away, if it's even possible at all. But with all of this change, many are starting to question again whether the government has a larger role in caring financially for people affected by job loss, especially with the increasing production and capital being generated by new automated systems.

Free Money?

Along with the rise of artificial intelligence, there is renewed interest in some form of a Universal Basic Income (UBI) to offset the potential losses from this revolution. The argument goes that if our new economy is driven by information technology and AI-based automation, there will be a growing chasm between the haves and have-nots. Proponents argue that this growing inequality must be addressed by society, specifically the federal government. The government should guarantee a basic level of income for all people to help those most affected by this economic shift that would help to meet basic needs like food, shelter, and medical care. This recognition of the dignity of all people and the desire to meet the needs of our neighbors is reminiscent of the greatest commandment in Matthew 22:37–39. But this is a fairly complex issue because of all of the factors involved, including the government's role in a free society, the cost of such a program, and how these type of programs might demotivate people from pursuing meaningful work in our changing society.

Countless books, articles, and discussions on this type of economic proposal expand on its potential dangers and benefits, so for our discussion, I want primarily to focus on how a UBI might affect a person on a character level. While a UBI might seem sensible, a hidden danger to this proposal relates to why we work and how work helps us live out the image of God. As we have already seen, we are created to work, and work is part of how God forms our character. One of the major objections to most UBI proposals is that they seem to disincentivize work. If all of your basic needs are met, why would you pursue meaningful and life-giving work?

Jay Richards explains that "we are tempted to be lazy, to avoid hard work, stress, and risk." He says that we are tempted to focus on our needs, rather than the needs of others, and to pursue short-term happiness rather than long-term gain.[10] This is a recognition of sin and its effect on our hearts, rather than an outright condemnation of a UBI. Sin distorts God's ideal and allows us to become more inwardly focused. Christians will rightfully disagree on the question of a UBI and should rigorously debate it in the public square so that we make the best decision for our nation and society. That debate should include a discussion of all of the contributing factors and of all of the potential impacts this kind of proposal will have on our society.

Regardless of your position on this issue, we know that no program or any amount of government can fix the underlying problem that we face as we look at how AI will affect our work and our lives. The story of creation teaches us that work is not just something that we do but is part of what it means to be a human made in God's image. Work is a good thing. But only the gospel message can change hearts and free us from sin.

GOSPEL CHANGE

The gospel is the message that nothing in this world defines us, because God has given us a new identity in Christ that trumps our sin and rebellion. Jesus paid the price for our rebellion and redeemed our souls from death. The impact of the gospel on our lives gives us a new outlook on the world around us. We approach our broken and sinful world knowing that God is going to redeem it and fix all that is wrong in it (Revelation 21).

Even though we have seen that work is not a product of the fall, we know from the Scriptures that our work is affected by our sin and rebellion. God cursed the ground because of our rebellion, and from it we reap the thorns and pains of work. But the gospel reminds us that even though we are tempted to put our trust and hope in our jobs—to make our jobs our identities—our true hope and identity are found in Jesus Christ alone.

You Are More Than What You Do

We are bombarded with the message that our worth and dignity come from what we do. We work longer hours and pursue new jobs because we are trying to make a name for ourselves or provide that extra bit of income to cover the bills. We work our fingers to the bone and at the end of the day believe that if we work hard, we will be saved from the toils of this life.

Devoid of the gospel, our world believes that we must do all that we can to make a name for ourselves in this life because there is nothing coming after it. We must pursue every opportunity to be remembered and make a mark on this world. Thus, our work becomes an idol for us and defines who we are. This is one of the many reasons that people often become depressed when they can't work or when they retire. We have built our lives around our work and let it define who we are, as opposed to letting God define who we are and being reminded that our work is meant to reflect God. We must remember that no amount of work or even the lack of work defines who we are. Our great God defines us.

When my grandmother was nearing the end of her life in 2015, she was ninety-four years old. She had taken care of me most of my childhood because both of my parents worked full-time jobs. I loved her more than anything in the world. As she was dying of old age in her hospital bed, I was reminded that even as she lay there motionless, unable to speak or even to open her eyes, she had the same value and dignity as the twenty-four-year-old tech giant who'd just invented the new big thing and the fifty-five-year-old CEO of a Fortune 500 company. Neither of those folks have more or less dignity because of what they can offer this world. While my grandmother, at that time, couldn't cook a meal, tell a good story, turn on a computer, or even lift her arm, she was worth more than any algorithm or robot will ever be. Not just because she was such a great woman (which she was) but because her great God made her in his image to reflect his glory. She reflected him through everything she did and how she loved others as herself.

My grandmother worked countless jobs throughout her life to make ends meet and to take care of her family, much like my grandfather and parents did. They adapted to their circumstances and did what was necessary to take care of their families and teach their children the value of hard work.

We Are Adaptable and Will Survive

It is becoming more common in society to talk about an apocalyptic future brought about by AI. We are driven by fear of the unknown, which causes us to overreact and forget the truths of God. The truth is that though we will encounter a future that is unknown to us, that future is not unknown to our God. God created all that we will ever know and created us to be like him. He not only knows the number of hairs on our heads (Luke 12:7), but he knows everything that the future holds. Nothing will get past him and nothing will ever surprise him because he is perfect in knowledge (Job 37:16). Regardless of how advanced AI may become, God is not fearful of our creations because he created us and everything that we have ever known.

God has created us to be able to adapt to our circumstances, to learn new skills, and to persevere when times are tough. This is one advantage that we have over current AI systems. These systems are wooden, unable to change disciplines or jobs without being reprogrammed. Humans are very different.

Think about all of the things that you do in a given day. I am a dad of two young boys, work a full-time job in research and communications, and am writing a book, all at the same time. I help my wife change diapers, prepare food, and give baths, as well as write articles, produce various resources, mow the lawn, fix the toilet, and maybe feed myself if I get a chance. The number of AI systems needed to replace me in all of my jobs is outrageously high. Until we develop general artificial intelligence or superintelligence, we are still more advanced than any AI system available, and that likely will be the case for decades and possibly centuries to come.

God is bigger than whatever we can create. God created all that we have ever known and nothing will catch him off guard (Ps. 139:7–10; Jer. 32:17). Not only that, but our value and dignity as God's image-bearers transcends our value for the things we can do. AI cannot change that, no matter how advanced it becomes.

Our adaptability is a part of what it means to be human, but it takes a lot of time and creative energy. We should welcome the challenge to adapt in the age of AI because AI tools will allow us to grow and mature in ways that aren't possible without their advances.

SHOULD WE FEAR THE FUTURE?

So should we fear the future? No. But we should be aware of how AI is changing our society. And as followers of Jesus, part of the message we are to share with our neighbors and communities is the fact that while we were created to work, our work doesn't define our dignity. God does. What he says about us is true regardless of what society tells us. We should not fear a future full of unknowns and change because of the God we serve (2 Tim. 1:7).

God is sovereign and our faith is not some delusion that helps us deal with the stresses of this life. Faith isn't a vain attempt to explain the unexplainable. As Hebrews 11:1 tells us, "faith is the assurance of things hoped for, the conviction of things not seen." Even though we don't know everything that the future holds, we know the one who holds the future in the palm of his hand. Our faith is a reminder that God is bigger and more powerful than anything we will ever create. No matter what, he is faithful to the end (1 Cor. 1:9).

CHAPTER 6

WAR

The New Battlefield

Like most Americans of the 1940s, my grandfather never planned on entering military service. He was a farmhand on his mother's multiacre farm in Alabama. He was a patriotic man who loved his family and his country. On September 16, 1940, the United States enacted the Selective Service and Training Act, which required all men from the ages of eighteen to sixty-five to register with the government to be drafted into service if needed as Germany's power grew in Europe. Dutifully, men from the big cities to the back roads across America registered and received their draft numbers. The numbers were based on a number of factors including age, dependents, and medical issues. Many hoped that the draft would never be needed, but on December 7, 1941, Japan attacked the US naval base at Pearl Harbor in Hawaii and the United States entered one of the bloodiest wars in the history of the world. This war forever changed our country, the world, and my grandfather's life.

My grandfather, who was twenty-two at the time, was bound to be drafted at some point because of the great need for men to fight. He was finally drafted in 1944 to serve as an infantryman. These brave men donned uniforms and underwent training at bases across the homeland before shipping off to battlefields in Europe and in the Pacific islands. Private First Class Roland Thacker left his young wife and daughter to journey across the Atlantic with countless men to push back the Germans who had taken much of Europe under their control. He was assigned to the 84th Infantry Division, 335th Regiment in Germany, where he served until the war ended.

I was always fascinated by his stories, which I heard growing up in and around his home. I spent countless days and weekends with my grandparents. He never told us many details from his tour of Europe, though. I often chalked this up to his fading memory, but later I realized that it was just too difficult for him to discuss. He'd lost many friends on the battlefields of Europe. While my grandfather was deployed, my grandmother held down the home front and tried to keep up with news from the war, just hoping that he would survive. Many newspapers ran stories of their hometown heroes and their valiant acts. My grandmother saved one clipping that chronicled one of the many heroic acts my grandfather performed in battle.

The headline of the news clipping reads, "Roland Thacker Gets Three out of Ten Germans." My grandfather was hailed as a hero for brave acts that helped protect Company G of the 335th Infantry. The article recounts how a squad of German infantrymen descended upon my grandfather as he and another solider were pinned down in a foxhole. He glanced out of the foxhole to see ten German soldiers coming toward them at full sprint. Immediately he began firing his Browning automatic rifle and took down two members of the German squad. The rest turned and fled. Then suddenly, a German machine gunner "blazed away" trying to take down the "stubborn Railsplitter." (Railsplitter was the nickname for members of the 84th Infantry Division.)

My grandfather was not scared so easily, though. His fellow solider was carrying an M-1 grenade launcher but was too afraid to use it. My grandfather grabbed the weapon and fired two rifle grenades at the machine gunner. The first fell short, but the second hit its mark. After that, the Germans gave up trying to take that foxhole. Granddaddy never thought twice about that heroic act.

He was awarded the Bronze Star medal, which I proudly inherited after he passed away in 2016 at the age of ninety-six. As I recall his life and service to the United States, I can't help but think of those two men in that foxhole. They were young and feared for their lives. My grandfather always downplayed how the other soldier acted when he told the story. To me, he did this because he knew that he felt the same way as that soldier did but wouldn't allow the fear to control him. He did what had to be done.

What if we could design a weapon that didn't experience fear and always performed its duty? What if we could design supersoldiers like robots that can fight on the front lines for us so that we don't have to send our men into harm's way? Or could we even create a cyberweapon that could be deployed to wreak havoc on an enemy's power grid or computer systems from thousands of miles away?

This isn't some future vision but a reality. Many of these tools exist in rudimentary form today, and soon our military engagements will look more like Hollywood movies and less like foxholes in Germany.

WEAPON TECHNOLOGY

Technology has been used in warfare since the beginning of time. Some of the earliest technology that humans developed was the bow and arrow. These arrows were made with stone tips and were primarily used for hunting and protection. Around the thirteenth century BC, we see the vast armies of Pharaoh, as told of in the book of Exodus. Egypt had great chariots and soldiers armed with these same bows. The following years didn't see very much technological development in warfare. Fast-forward to the time of Christ, the Romans helped to pioneer other advances in warfare like swords, catapults, and spears.

Around the ninth century AD, the Chinese are said to have developed gunpowder, which revolutionized war. By year 1000, we see the first piece of technology to be called a gun, which was a bamboo tube that fired a spear. Around 1250, cannons and siege guns were developed, which led to more portable cannons and later to what we now recognize as a gun.

By the American Civil War in 1861, the first automated weapon was devised by Richard Gatling, which drastically sped up the firing and reloading of a gun. This Gatling gun was a vast improvement over musket-style rifles because it allowed four men to do as much damage as a hundred on the battlefield. This automated gun combined six to ten barrels on one weapon and was operated by a hand crank.

Gatling's plan for this gun was to save human lives. Paul Scharre in his book *Army of None* references a letter from Gatling to a friend in which he describes his motivation for building the new weapon: "It occurred to me that if I could invent a machine—a gun—which could by its rapidity of fire enable one man to do as much battle duty as a hundred, that it would, to a great extent, supersede the necessity of large armies, and consequently, exposure to battle and disease be greatly diminished."[1]

Gatling's motivation was pure in the sense that he wanted to see fewer men engaged in war, but history shows that this technological development led to more bloodshed. It was used in some of the bloodiest wars in history to inflict maximum damage on the battlefield. This automated weapon revolutionized modern warfare and led to the development of the modern machine gun, one of which my grandfather valiantly destroyed in that German forest. But little did my grandfather know on that day in 1945 that the machine gun would soon be considered outdated technology and that just as the war ended, computer developments were already being discussed by the pioneers of artificial intelligence. What Gatling started with the very first automated weapon soon led to the development of semi-autonomous drone warfare and missile defense systems capable of engaging nuclear warheads.

THOU SHALL NOT KILL

The Bible makes it clear that the taking of another human life is a serious matter. In Genesis 4, we read of the first person to be murdered. Cain and Abel were the first two sons of Adam and Eve. One day in the field, Cain killed Abel because it infuriated him that the Lord chose Abel's offering over his offering. When the Lord questioned Cain about his brother's death, Cain questioned the Lord and said that he did not know where his brother was. Then the Lord responded to Cain, "What have you done? The voice of your brother's blood is crying to me from the ground" (Gen. 4:10).

Cain was required to account for what he had done to his brother. He was punished by God because the taking of another's life is an assault on the dignity of that image-bearer. The taking of another's life is a grievous sin and one that ultimately will be punished. This dignity extends even to our enemies, because they too are created in the image of God. Because of our sin and rebellion against God, we ushered in the age of destruction, war, death, sickness, and brokenness and the natural order of things turned upside down. God's creations also turned on each other, committing murder and devising war.

GOVERNMENT AND THE SWORD

God calls his people to pursue justice for wrongs committed against our fellow image-bearers. The prophet Isaiah proclaims that we are to "cease to do evil, learn to do good; seek justice, correct oppression; bring justice to the fatherless, plead the widow's cause" (Isa. 1:16–17). We pursue these things because every human being is created in God's image and no one has the right to demean, oppress, or kill another person. While we don't seek to engage in war or bloodshed, seeking justice is one of the many ways that we can image God. God is just and his people are to seek to be like him (Ps. 37:28).

But one of the questions that arises out of a quest for justice is who is to pursue it: individuals or governments? Individuals obviously are called to pursue justice within their own circles and lives, but governments also have a role in our society as designed by God. Paul tells us in Romans 13:1 that "there is no authority except from God, and those that exist have been instituted by God." God is the ultimate authority and ruler of the universe. Nothing happens outside of his reign and rule. Governments have only the authority that God gives to them.

So that means government is designed to pursue justice for the common good, even as it is made up of sinful and broken people who do not always prioritize and pursue justice. While government will inevitably fail us, the failure does not thwart God's good plan for ultimate justice. Human governments are designed specifically to have limited power, meaning they do not have ultimate authority as God does (Rom. 13:4).

Governments around the world have different levels of authority and power, but none will ever rival God's authority as the creator of the universe. The role of government is to protect its citizens, pursue justice, uphold liberty, and promote human flourishing. One of the ways this takes place is through military defense and war. But is war something we should even engage in?

A JUST WAR?

Some take the assault on human dignity to mean that all war is unjust because we are not allowed to take another's life regardless of what they do. This pacifist position is popular in some faith traditions, even Christianity. To be a pacifist, one abstains from war and any type of combat. But one of the difficult things to align with a pacifist position is how we are to seek justice for the oppressed and those who have been killed by others. The flip side to the pacifist position is one that is extremely popular in parts of the world: militarism. Militarism is simply the position that we should maintain a strong military capability but also be prepared to use it to defend or expand national interests. Many in this camp support military engagement at any cost and often overlook the great cost of war.

While not all wars are just, war itself is not something to be avoided if the war is in line with the role that the government has been given by God. A Christian understanding of just war was first promoted by Augustine of Hippo based on his understanding of Romans 13:4.[2] Paul proclaims that the government is to carry out "God's wrath on the wrongdoer." Augustine developed just-war theory to lay out how a war is to be carried out if it is necessary to uphold God's design for government.

Just-war theory explains that the only just cause for war is the protection of peace and the punishment of the wicked. For a war to be just, it is not to be pursued gleefully but as a last resort. Thus, people and nations should neither engage in war lightly nor abstain from it, because war can be used to seek justice for the oppressed. Another key insight into a just war is proportionality. This means that the good gained from the war must outweigh the evil that is sustained. War always has casualties, damages, and costs. This concept of proportionality also extends to the use of certain weapons in war, meaning that any response must be in proportion to the initial assault. Proportionality and justice are the main reasons that mustard gas has been banned internationally. The gas was popularized in World War I, but could not be contained when deployed. The gas would be blown by the wind and often poisoned noncombatants too.

The use of nuclear weapons is a hotly debated topic, even among Christians, on grounds of proportionality. Nuclear weapons wreak such havoc and cause so much death that some people find it hard to justify their use. Others argue that they may be used only as a last resort, as in the way they were used to end the Pacific campaign of World War II to save countless lives. The United States is the only nation to have used a nuclear weapon in war. Other nations have developed the weapons for themselves, often in the name of defense. But some stockpile these weapons of mass destruction to gain notoriety and power on the world stage.

The type of weaponry used in war has both moral and ethical components to it. Military applications of AI are often controversial and complex because they raise a host of moral and ethical concerns, including the role humans play as these systems engage enemies. Many people understandably disagree on the best tools to be used in warfare. However, this disagreement does not absolve us of the need for reflection and consideration because real human lives are at stake. Most people would agree that the use of rifles, airplanes, and vehicular weapons is permitted, but does that include weapons where humans are less involved in their use? Is AI ushering in a new age of warfare with semi-autonomous and soon fully autonomous weapons?

AI WEAPONS

As early as World War II, the United States employed a host of new weaponry like rockets, missiles, and bombs. These tools were very effective when used properly. They were able to extend the range of targeting for the military but were not very accurate. In 1943, the first successful precision-guided munition (PGM) was developed by the Germans, called the Falcon torpedo. This innovation was equipped with an acoustic homing seeker, which helped steer the torpedo toward ships and detonated it when it reached them.[3] A German U-boat launching the torpedo would have to go completely silent to keep the torpedo from turning around and attacking it.

These munitions were unable to be recalled once they launched and had very little autonomy. After these basic PGMs were developed, newer homing weapons soon followed that could track moving objects. It is important to note that homing weapons are not able to select or engage targets on their own authority. Humans are very involved in the decision-making process.

The human decision-making role is often portrayed on a loop called OODA, which has four stages: observe, orient, decide, act. This loop was developed by military strategist and United States Air Force Colonel John Boyd for use in all military operations. In homing munitions, the human is in the loop, deciding what to engage and when.

But newer weapons systems equipped with AI are beginning to replace the human in the decision-making loop. As decision making is increasingly augmented or automated, humans will become less and less involved because of the speed at which decisions will have to be made.

Automation is now being used in these systems to search out, identify, track, and prioritize targets.[4] This increasingly puts the human "on the loop" or "out of the loop." On-the-loop systems are very common in today's military technology.

These systems include ship-based defense systems like the US Aegis combat system and land-based systems like the US Patriot missiles. They operate independent of humans, but a human is able to intervene at any time if the system malfunctions or makes a bad decision. Out-of-the-loop systems can be described as fully autonomous weapons. They can perform most operational tasks, but a human being is still ultimately in control of the system. But how long will this level of control last as AI systems become faster and faster? Will humans be able to retain control for much longer?

Even today we have systems that border on full autonomy or cross that line. Israel has one such drone weapon, named Harpy, which was deployed in 2004. The Harpy system is considered a loitering munition, which means it has a target area and can engage targets within it as it sees fit. The system is controlled by a form of artificial intelligence that does not need a human's approval to engage targets. In 2019, Israel Aerospace Industries announced a brand new mini-Harpy, which combines the capabilities of the company's two main loitering munitions, the Harop and the Harpy, in a smaller package. These new systems have already been sold to numerous nations like China, India, South Korea, and Turkey.

South Korea also has a sentry gun deployed in the demilitarized zone between itself and North Korea which is said to be able to cross from semi-autonomous to fully autonomous mode as needed.[5] The semi and fully autonomous modes employ complex forms of artificial intelligence, and this is only the beginning. AI-based weapons are not just part of a sci-fi movie plot, they are part of real life and are already defending our borders and skies. The question is not whether fully autonomous systems are possible but where the responsibility for their use lies and how these systems should be used in a just war and for defense.

HUMAN RESPONSIBILITY

In *Army of None,* Paul Scharre writes, "Humans are not perfect, but they can empathize with their opponents and see the bigger picture. Unlike humans, autonomous weapons would have no ability to understand the consequences of their actions, no ability to step back from the brink of war."[6]

Scharre couldn't be more right. Human beings are not at all perfect. We make bad decisions and we are often influenced by our environments more than we think. Scripture tells us that all people are fallen (Rom. 3:23) and that our fallenness extends to our decision-making capabilities. We fail and make mistakes every day, but often our mistakes and faulty judgments have very little impact on the people around us. But failure in war or in a military engagement can within minutes or even seconds lead to massive loss of life or start an international conflict, because AI is already controlling many of our weapons systems today. AI systems can engage faster and more accurately than their human operators. Just take the mini-Harpy system, which can respond to a threat within seconds rather than wait on a human to engage the system.[7]

But God has uniquely positioned us to be morally responsible for our neighbor, especially when they are facing injustice, oppression, or abuse. Our machines will never be capable of holding that responsibility. This is one of the flaws in the argument that humans are simply machines. If we are simply machines, then logically we should design systems to bear the weight and responsibilities of these types of

decisions. But God designed the universe with only one creature that is capable of bearing this responsibility. Humans
are not machines and machines can
never become human. We alone are *God has uniquely positioned*
responsible to care for the least of *us to be morally responsible*
these and to pursue justice for all. *for our neighbor. Machines*

When we are seeking to apply *will never be capable of*
wisdom to our development and *bearing that responsibility.*
application of weapons in war, we
must keep these truths central in our pursuit. Nothing we will
ever create with our hands can bear the weight of the calling
God has given us. Every man, woman, and child in the world
is created in the image of God, and this includes our enemies.
We alone will give an account before God for how we honored
him and loved our neighbors through the use of these tools.

AI is neither good nor bad in itself, but a tool that God
has given us to use with wisdom. For example, AI can be used
for good in strengthening target systems so that they are
more accurate when used in long-range missiles and drones.
These advancements allow us to minimize accidentally killing
innocents while engaging an enemy. Advancements can also
be used to protect soldiers and keep them out of harm's way.
But using these tools can also have unintended consequences.

Even with advanced weapons systems like drones, which
use more precise computer-aided targeting, the United States
Pentagon said in 2018 that "no one will ever know" how many
innocent lives have been lost during the fight against the
Islamic State and Syria.[8] These tools are not one hundred
percent accurate. They fail. They fail because they are created
by fallen humans and operate in a fallen world. Even as specific
numbers vary on the number of innocent lives lost in war, many

argue the number of human casualties is less than it would be without the drones because they reduce the need for ground troops and the systems are more accurate than previous target systems driven in large part by fallible humans.[9]

At least for the time being, US military engagements will have a human in the decision-making loop per the Department of Defense in 2017.[10] But that directive may not last if other countries and groups start to use more autonomous weapons, because we might not be able to adequately defend against their speed and accuracy without using autonomous weapons ourselves.

But shirking our responsibility to enact justice by passing it on to automated systems reveals a lack of concern for the human beings affected by our decisions in our desire for a quick ending to combat.

For all of their good, a major and often overlooked danger of AI-empowered weapons is our tendency to dehumanize our enemies. Using AI weapons, we do not come near to those we engage in combat and don't often think of them as men and women with families, livelihoods, hopes, and dreams. We see our enemies and often our own troops merely as data on the virtual battlefield. They are blips on a screen rather than flesh-and-blood human beings. AI can desensitize us to the reality that in war, real human lives are lost.

PURSUING JUSTICE IN A PLURALISTIC SOCIETY

Major technology companies routinely work with the government on various projects. These range from weapons systems to the development of AI-empowered tools. In 2018 and 2019, employees and engineers at Google and Microsoft refused to work on certain US Department of Defense (DoD) projects because the employees decided that working on systems that could be used in war and bloodshed violated their consciences.

For example, Google had partnered with the DoD to develop an AI-based image-recognition program called the Algorithmic Warfare Cross-Function Team, or simply Project Maven. Project Maven was designed to identify enemy targets on the battlefield. The AI system processes massive amount of video data captured everyday by US military drones and reports to military and civilian analysts potential targets for military engagement.

Google employees protested their involvement in the program, arguing that Google should not be in the business of war since the company's historic slogan has been "Do no evil." In April 2018, thousands of Google's employees, including many senior engineers, signed a letter to CEO Sundar Pichai in protest of Google's involvement in Project Maven.[11] In June 2018, Google announced that it would not renew the government contract for Project Maven amid the outcry from its employees and many people in the technology field. Employees rejoiced at this decision, but some criticized the move, arguing that dropping the research would increase the likelihood of war and civilian deaths. Those who criticized Google's decision included Amazon founder and CEO Jeff Bezos, who claimed that "if big tech companies are going to turn their back on the US Department of Defense, this country is going to be in trouble."[12]

The ethical application of AI weapons systems is a hotly debated topic, as it should be. We should never encourage the use of AI in military applications without deep reflection on the implications of its use and whether it will uphold the dignity of all people as we pursue justice.

In July 2018, 2,400 AI researchers and practitioners signed a pledge to block the development of fully autonomous weapons systems because of the massive moral and ethical implications of the technology.[13] Signers included the founder of Google DeepMind, which developed the famous AlphaGo system, as well as SpaceX CEO Elon Musk. For them killer robots and fully autonomous weapons systems cross a moral line because the decision to kill is moved from the human being to the machine.

While I hear, understand, and largely agree with the concerns raised by Google and others about AI weapons, I fear the lack of development of these weapons will do more harm than good. These tools should be used as deterrents against rogue states and groups. It's a question not of whether this technology will be created and used but of who will create it and how they will use it.

CONCLUSION

So how should we think about the use of artificial intelligence in warfare? John F. Kennedy once said, "It is an unfortunate fact that we can secure peace only by preparing for war."[14] Part of living in a broken society is the fact that there are bad actors on the international stage who must be engaged if we are to live in a peaceful society. While Christians should be the first to warn of the horrors of war and how war can dehumanize our neighbors, we should also be the first to champion the dignity and worth of all people as we seek to enact justice for evils committed.

Scripture calls us to engage in the mission of justice, rather than to sit passively by waiting for others to fight our battles for us. But we also need to be aware of the temptation to pursue militarism as some type of patriotic duty. Along with most of the Christian church throughout history, we seek to stand against the oppressors, championing the dignity of all people and pursuing justice. This concept of just war must be the basis for how we think about military engagement in the age of AI.

It is not a question of whether AI will be used in warfare; it already is and will continue to be part of the weaponry that we employ. But AI must be wielded with wisdom and should never be used as an excuse to disengage from our responsibility to love God and love our neighbor. We need to be reminded that we will be held responsible for how justice

Scripture calls us to engage in the mission of justice, rather than to sit passively by waiting for others to fight our battles for us.

is enacted, giving an account of our deeds one day before the judgment seat of God. Decisions about the use of artificial intelligence in war should never be made in a vacuum, because they have real-world implications on people created in the image of God.

AI weapons are ubiquitous in today's military and will be used increasingly in life-and-death situations. Fully autonomous weapons might just be a few programming steps removed from reality, and we must be thoughtful and concerned about how these new weapons will revolutionize and reinvent the battlefield. These conversations are not just for military leaders or politicians. They are for everyday people. Our brothers, sisters, moms, and dads serve with pride, just as my grandfather did. The decisions we make today as a society affect not only how we engage on the international stage but also how our loved ones are protected as they serve. Our decisions as a nation and as a people will reveal our understanding of human dignity and our belief that all people are created in the image of God.

CHAPTER 7

DATA AND PRIVACY

You Are the Product

To little fanfare and even less press coverage, the internet went from a military and government project to a publicly available tool on August 6, 1991. If you are old enough to remember the days before the internet, you probably didn't even know that this world-shifting tool went live. Most people had no clue. The beginnings of the public internet were pretty rough. It was difficult to navigate because search engines didn't really appear until 1993 and Google wasn't even founded until 1998. Early search engines were extremely unreliable and it was pretty easy to game the system to get your site in front of people, even if it had nothing to do with someone's search.

Early search engines utilized simple algorithms to produce search results. These algorithms calculated the page ranking of a website in search results by the number of times that your search term appeared on that page. It was extremely easy to game the system and artificially boost your website by adding lines of popular search terms on your site. Some sites even listed the same word in white on a white background to fool the search engines. The first major search engines I remember using as a kid were AltaVista and Yahoo, both founded in 1995. But I will always have a fond place in my heart for a 1997 classic called Ask Jeeves.

Ask Jeeves was different because it was designed for users to ask a full question in everyday language instead of typing just a search term. It could also organize search results around common questions that people asked online. Most people even used punctuation when searching (or at least I did), which seems quaint with the rise of emojis and txtng language made up of half-typed words and dropped vowels. Jeeves was a "gentleman's personal gentleman" or valet, who appeared on the homepage in a full suit always ready to assist you by answering any question you asked him. Ask Jeeves' unique twist of organizing the results based on questions helped users navigate the results and find what they were looking for quickly.

Google was founded in 1998 by Sergey Brin and Larry Page. They brought another twist to how we searched the ever-expanding worldwide web. Brin and Page realized how easy it was for people to alter search results and how unreliable the results often were. They devised a new type of algorithm that crawled to the ends of the internet and ranked pages based on how many times a site was referenced by another site. Think of an academic paper that you wrote in school. You were required to cite a number of sources for your claims and data. In Brin and Page's citation method, the more a page was cited by other sites, the more reliable that content was thought to be. This shift in thinking led to Google's breakout success, by mid-2018 turning a small startup into the world's premier search engine worth more than $110.8 billion.

WHAT IS DATA?

To say that $110.8 billion is a lot of money might be the understatement of this entire book. But what might surprise you is that Google's value today is not really about the revolutionary way it pulls search results. It is all about the data that companies like Google collect on each of us every day and how that data is used. Data can be a powerful tool for good, but misuse of it can devastate people's lives. It seems like every day there is a new use for personal data and new ways that it is being tracked. Data collection and analysis is not a new discipline, but we now have tools to collect and analyze almost every conceivable type of data about people and the world around us. Data is most often analyzed and used to market products and services to us, where companies like Google sell predictive products based on the data collected on us to marketers and other companies.

Often, we think of data only in terms of digital data and tracking, but data is simply observations about the world that God has created. Humanity has always tracked data in some way or another. Every observation that we make about the world and other people is tracked in our minds. This is how we form opinions and encounter an ever-changing world. We collect this data based on personal experiences and through the observations of others. And we process this data to make our daily lives easier.

Take for example agricultural data. My paternal grandparents were avid gardeners most of their lives. My grandfather was born and raised on a farm in rural Alabama, near where my grandmother was raised. Both of their families had massive farms, and they both worked them for many years.

My grandfather learned much of his knowledge about how to garden from his parents and their parents before them. He worked full time outside in agriculture until his late eighties and then retired to continue cultivating his own garden. My grandmother was known for her beautiful flower gardens, and when my wife and I bought their house after their deaths, we had our work cut out for us taming the gardens and flower beds. Neither of us has a green thumb. We lack the knowledge and insights my grandparents learned from observing the world.

My grandparents tracked the rainfall, the soil pH levels, and the amount of sun their plants and flowers received. They used this data to grow healthy and more plentiful crops. Our world is full of data, and we can track nearly everything in it: the weather, animal behavior, the stars, and anything we search for online. Data collection takes place all the time, and you are likely pretty comfortable knowing that some of the data about you is being tracked. But most people become uneasy with someone else knowing intimate details of their lives. Often this uneasiness arises from the exploitation of that data for personal or financial gain. But more on that later.

My grandparents were reflecting the image of God as they sought to grow vegetables in their garden. You and I also reflect the image of God as we make observations about the world around us. Part of our image-bearing capacity is the ability to observe the universe and use that knowledge to further our dominion over the earth and to care for society. These observations allow us to adapt to the world around us and reorient our plans to better fit with the way that the world was designed.

DATA COLLECTION

Data collection happens every day. Nearly everything you do in the digital world is tracked by someone or something. Data drives the algorithms that Amazon uses to recommend a new book or product to you. It drives how Netflix is able to recommend a perfect show. You likely delight in the fact that your phone gives you a shortcut to your digital wallet when you arrive at Starbucks for your morning coffee. I particularly like that my email service gives me suggested responses to emails that make answering the onslaught of messages I get each day easier. It isn't always correct, but it often saves me some time.

Online data tracking normally entails your likes, dislikes, recent purchases, and personal data you input when you sign up for various services. But it also includes searches you are too embarrassed to tell another living soul about. You might be embarrassed to ask a friend about your marriage troubles or why your kids act out. You might be ashamed of your pornography addiction and google how to overcome a porn problem. You might wonder why you feel so lonely even though you have so many friends on social media and connections on LinkedIn. What you wouldn't admit to someone else, you will tell Google, and that information is being constantly tracked.

But before you decide to leave the grid completely and

convert your assets into gold bars buried near a remote cabin in the woods, like Ron Swanson on *Parks and Recreation,* you need to understand that much of the data collected on you is often depersonalized and used to enrich your life. Data is stored in massive data farms all across the world. It is often processed by a form of artificial intelligence that picks up on patterns and connections that allow companies to make informed decisions about what you like and dislike, as well as factors that might lead you to click on a certain link or buy a new product.

Prior to online tracking, data was often collected about our behaviors through surveys and observations. That data often was cataloged in some fashion but sat unused because of limited resources and manpower. Many companies today are drowning in data with no hope of ever being able to use it properly. Data scientist Seth Stephens-Davidowitz explains, "They have lots of terabytes, but few major insights. The size of a database, I believe, is frequently overrated. . . . The bigger the effects [of an insight], the fewer the number of observations necessary to see it."[1]

He explains that you need to touch a hot stove only once to realized that it can hurt you, but you might need to drink coffee a thousand times to determine whether it gives you headaches. "The intensity of its impact shows up quickly with so little data." The truth is that we don't need most of the data that is collected on us each day. No one does. But companies and organizations don't know what they don't know, so they tend to overcollect in the hope of being able to use it one day for a major insight. But before we see the impact of data collection on our lives, we need to explore another way data is so powerful and why we feel like we never have enough.

STRIVING TO BE GOD

From the beginning of time, humans have sought to be God and to rule our own lives. The first sin was essentially Adam and Eve's telling God that it wasn't enough to be like him but that they must be gods themselves, knowing good and evil. We long to be gods in our own right because of pride and arrogance. We want to control everything about our lives from our jobs to our families. We want the world to be built just for us and to cater to our every need.

AI can help humanity fulfill one of our most dangerous and sinful longings—to be gods over the world around us. But we can also use the power of AI systems and the data we capture to honor God and love our neighbor. Using technology, we are able to know things that no one has ever seen before, such as what part of our DNA might cause us to develop lung cancer later in life or whether, based on our size and skill, we are likely to be talented athletes. Given enough data, we might even predict world-shaping events with greater accuracy. With the right data and the AI to process it, we can begin to see relationships between things like never before in human history.

With the power of AI, we can harness data to control our environments. Smart thermostats can adjust the temperature of our homes even before we think that it is getting too cold. We can allow our news sources to control everything that we see and hear (effectively creating echo chambers of our own views). We can analyze data sources to see how certain copy, design, and time of day affects our purchasing habits so that companies can manipulate us to increase the likelihood of our purchasing their latest gadgets, devices, or services. We can use these advances for the glory of God, but often use them to indulge our sinful and prideful hearts instead.

The power of AI and modern technology can fool us into thinking that we are something that we are not. That we are in control. That we are mini gods.

While this power might feel good and helpful in the moment, in the long term, our creaturely status will catch up with us. We will realize that for all of our planning and analyzing, we cannot predict or know all things. We will be disappointed and burned out by the vain pursuit of power and knowledge—power and knowledge we were never created to hold. We will see our natural limitations but still strive for more.

Scripture is full of examples illustrating the vanity and sinful pursuit of being gods. But one that stands out to me the most is the story of the exodus. God's chosen people, the nation of Israel, were brought to Egypt by God's sovereign hand because of a famine in their land. Joseph's brothers sold him into slavery, but God used their sin to save his people (Gen. 50:2). Joseph ruled under Pharaoh as one of the most powerful people in the world. As the book of Exodus begins, we read that a new king came to power in Egypt who did not know Joseph. This Pharaoh sought to control the nation of Israel and lord his power over them. But the more that Pharaoh sought to exert his power over them, the more they multiplied and grew. The Egyptians became uneasy at Israel's size and power.

At the appointed time, God raised up a new leader who would set his people free. Pharaoh's heart was hardened by God, and no matter how much Pharaoh sought to control Israel or to keep the Israelites from leaving Egypt, he was unable to stop God's plan. As we read in Exodus 7–12, Pharaoh sought to be God and to use everything at his disposal to counteract the plagues from God. But to no avail. No matter Pharaoh's power, ingenuity, or cunning, God's plan was never thwarted. Pharaoh tried to use his knowledge, his people, and his military to stop the Israelites from leaving Egypt, but God never let his people down. God rescued them from the plagues, the pursuit of Pharaoh's army, and even the waters of the Red Sea.[2]

This story is one of the foundational stories in the Scriptures that God uses to remind his people of his love for them, his power to defeat the greatest powers in the world, and his knowledge of all things. Nothing could stop God from executing his plan to save his people, not even Pharaoh.

So what does Exodus have to do with data and artificial intelligence? AI tools can fool us into thinking that we can be all knowing, all powerful, and gods in our own right just as Pharaoh falsely believed. They can lead us to believe that with the right data, right algorithm, or enough human ingenuity, we can solve the world's problems and even beat death itself. As we noted in chapter 2, futurists like Yuval Noah Harari claim that based on humanity's record of containing diseases, combatting famine, and controlling war, we will be able to turn our efforts and godlike power to the issues of death and happiness. He argues that we will overcome because we finally have the tools and the power to achieve the unthinkable.

In the short term, Pharaoh felt as though he was all powerful because he was able to stop the nation who claimed to be God's chosen people from leaving Egypt. He relished his control over the Israelites and desired to be a god. But with plague after plague and sign after sign, God proclaimed that he was the only God and that no one, regardless of knowledge or supposed power, could be God. There is only one God, and we are to honor him above all things (Deut. 6:4; 1 Cor. 8:5–6).

DATA ABUSED

It is easy to see how data can be misused and abused in a fallen world. Since data collection and storage is relatively cheap compared with past generations, our society will continue to overcollect data in the hope of discovering some new insight, typically to increase profits or change human behavior. Big data can mean big profits for companies that use it well. But big data can also be used to belittle, manipulate, or devalue our neighbor in the pursuit of the almighty dollar.

Bad Data and Faulty Humans

In the summer of 2015, a young man from Brooklyn checked his Google Photos app and made a horrifying observation. Google Photos is an app that can be used on a smart phone and computers to store and organize the endless amounts of photos that we take each day. Many photo applications employ an image-recognition system powered by AI that automatically tags your photos for you. These systems can categorize photos based on events, people, and places.

When this African-American man opened his photo application, he discovered that it had labeled a picture of him and his friend as gorillas. Obviously, this was a bug or glitch in the system, but the fact that the AI labeled someone of color this way is unacceptable. Google quickly removed the label from the system and promised to fix the issue moving forward. But why did this situation even occur in the first place?

AI systems are often taught to perform certain actions based on training data and repetition. Data bias, as in the case of the photo application, can occur for a multitude of reasons, but often because of a lack of data or skewed data. If image-recognition software is fed thousands of images of light-skinned people, the system will learn to distinguish between faces of light-skinned people quickly and pick up on subtle differences. In the case of Google Photos, it seems that the system was not fed a diverse set of data, which led to its falsely labeling African-Americans as gorillas. While the system wasn't designed to exhibit bias, it picked up on these patterns through the data it was trained on. The failure was in the system, but the responsibility lay with those who created it. The system wasn't aware of what it was doing; it was just processing data based on how it was taught.

Another reason why an AI system might exhibit bias and discrimination is if it gives answers to a question in a way that a human might not understand. A human programmer may give an AI a set of solid data and certain directions on what it wants the AI to do, but often the AI system will perform these tasks in ways that humans wouldn't think of.

Take for example an AI program from Stanford and Google that was tasked with building a digital map of an area. Digital maps are part of most popular navigation systems, like Waze and Google Maps. The AI was designed to take a satellite image of an area, turn it into a Google map drawing, and then turn the drawing back into a satellite image.[3] This was to see how advanced the AI was and how it could be used to automate this process in the future. The human programmers assumed the system would make the digital drawing of the map and then recreate a satellite-like image from it.

In theory, this tool could save countless hours and resources, all the while speeding up the updating of maps to add new developments and so on.

But the AI did something that astonished its designers. It recreated a nearly perfect replica of the original satellite image, which caused developers to question what was going on. They found that the system "hid" the image data from the original image in the map version in a way that would be impossible for a human being to pick up on. It did this to achieve the goal it was given to remake the satellite image; it just did it in a way that the human handlers didn't plan for or think about.

Was the AI trying to trick or deceive a human being? No, the system wasn't conscious or trying to be deceitful. It just found a quicker and more efficient way to accomplish its goal within the rules it was given. The AI didn't fail. Humans did. The system performed its task perfectly. But as AI is used to control more and more things in our society, we need to realize that these tools hold enormous power over our lives and society. We must be aware not only of their benefits but also of their limitations and their potential to disrupt our society.

Life-Altering Bias

AI systems are increasingly being used to make decisions that carry a lot more weight than just labeling photos and drawing maps. In October 2018, Amazon scrapped an AI system that it used to evaluate job candidates after it was discovered that the system was favoring male candidates over female candidates. One can easily see how this type of discrimination could lead to life-altering bias, because some very talented women could be denied jobs based on how an AI system processed their resumes.

You may have heard about how AI is increasingly being used in home-loan-application processing and decisions. According to a Fannie Mae survey released in October 2018, more than one quarter (27 percent) of all mortgage lenders use a form of AI in their mortgage business. In 2020, 58 percent of all mortgage lenders are expected to use AI to make the process easier for the company and for customers.[4] This technology can also be used to spot fraud more quickly and speed up the time it takes to get approval.

Where could this go wrong?

My wife and I just purchased a new home. But before we were able to put an offer on the house, we had to be approved for our home loan. A number of factors play into the decision to give us a loan. How old are we? Where do I work? Does my wife work outside the home? How much debt do we have? Where do we want to buy? What is our credit score?

But what about the crime rate of the area we are wanting to buy in? What about the color of our skin? What about the opportunities that I was afforded based on where I grew up and how I was raised? How could these seemingly small factors play into the process?

If we were denied our loan, I naturally would go to my banker and demand to know the reason. You would too. Increasingly, though, your banker might not know why you were denied. Because AI systems make decisions without direct human oversight, homebuyers and their bankers might not be able to see why the AI denied the loan. These systems are designed to maximize profit and protect the liability of companies, but they can go too far. Should they deny nonwhite applicants at higher rates than white applicants? You would say no, but this may become more of a reality than you think.

Everyday these systems produce results that we trust, but as a society we must evaluate the results with an eye for equality and equal access.

HUMAN RESPONSIBILITY

If you are concerned about how data is being used and abused, you are not alone. To many people, living in a society where data is always being collected on them feels more like Big Brother than Mayberry. Governments and companies have been under immense pressure in the last few years to do something about the ways that data on us is being harvested. From the European Union's privacy act, called the GDPR (General Data Protection Regulation), to the renewed emphasis on transparency by companies like Apple, there are some hopeful signs that these issues are being addressed. While you might not agree with every detail of these regulations or plans, there is a common theme that we should all agree on. In the age of AI, human responsibility will be paramount to human flourishing.

Of the many temptations that we have addressed in this book so far, the temptation to shirk human responsibility and oversight may be one of the most important issues for us to address in our lifetimes. As AI becomes more and more advanced, taking on responsibilities in increasingly weighty areas like job applications, home loans, medical care, and others, we must not pass the responsibility for decision making and its repercussions to our creations. In the last chapter, we addressed human responsibility in terms of a human being in the loop, especially for life-and-death situations related to war. But this emphasis on responsibility must extend past military engagement and into our living rooms and work environments.

The area of criminal justice provides a vivid example of why we must remain engaged and responsible for decisions that are increasingly being automated.

In 2011, Shai Danziger, Jonathan Levav, and Liora Avnaim-Pesso released a major study on Israeli judges and their sentencing patterns. Their research found that judges are more likely to give lenient or lighter sentencing in the early mornings or after an extended break, such as lunch.[5] Why might this be the case? Because the judgment of human beings can be affected by outside and unrelated factors such as hunger, fatigue, and stress. But what if we could use a system that never experienced those factors and ruled similarly each time without breaks? AI can analyze more data than humans and never grows tired.

The temptation to shirk human responsibility and oversight may be one of the most important issues for us to address in our lifetimes.

The American criminal justice system in 2018 held nearly 2.3 million people.[6] That means about one in 150 people in the US was incarcerated. Governments around the world are exploring what it might look like if AI were used in sentencing reform, such as the use of systems like COMPAS (Correctional Offender Management Profiling for Alternative Sanctions), which serves as a case-management and decision-support tool. AI programs could be used to comb through data on a person, their community, and their environment to predict the likelihood of their recommitting an offense and also helping to set the length of their sentences if they are convicted. This use of AI has enormous benefits in situations like this because it can allow for more factors to be included in decision making.

But the use of AI also has detrimental effects if used incorrectly. As we have already seen, our data can be skewed or biased. What if an AI was giving shorter sentences to those with lighter skin and longer sentences to darker skinned people? What if the prisoners in the COMPAS example were given different sentences based solely on where they were from, rather than on the crime they committed or their efforts to reform during their incarceration? While we can address some of these biases in the data collected and analyzed, our society must commit to keeping AI tools in their proper place. It would be easy to shirk our responsibilities because we falsely believe that machines are unbiased or will be fairer than the average human being.

We should hold fast to the idea that tools are just that—tools to aid us, not replace us, in doing our jobs and carrying out our responsibilities to care for our neighbors and execute earthly justice for wrongdoings, to love God and love our neighbor as ourselves. We must bear those weighty responsibilities as God's image-bearers.

WHAT IS PRIVACY?

In the last few years, many people around the world have become aware of just how powerful data can be and are rightfully nervous about how it is being collected on them. Though some of this data allows us to live more comfortably because it is used to improve our lives, data has a dark side. It can be manipulated and used to denigrate ourselves and our neighbor. It can be used to undermine society and our privacy.

Data played a major role in the outcome of the last few presidential elections, especially 2016. From Facebook's user data being harnessed by Cambridge Analytica to target people for politically motivated ads without their consent to the spread of Russian misinformation campaigns, many people woke to the reality of the power of data.

While most do not approve of digital manipulation tactics and the use of fake news to influence our elections, some issues surrounding data usage are extremely controversial and not as clean cut as we often like. Take for example the California law-enforcement officials who used DNA samples from family-tree databases to solve the thirty-year-old Golden State murder case. Officials were able to obtain DNA sample results from 23andMe for use in this investigation.

Was this an invasion of privacy? While the data was not personalized, it was used to track down a relative of the Golden State murderer. While you may feel that this use of data was right because it brought justice to a murderer, the same case can make you feel uncomfortable because officials were able to use data from a private company to track someone down. Should officials be granted access to private information for any type of criminal case? Just homicide cases? Who decides?

I feel uneasy about living in a big brother state, but I'm also thankful that this man is off the streets and being judged for his crimes. The tension is real in many privacy-related cases.

You may even have your own fears that your device is listening to you or recording you. As I sit in a coffee shop working on this chapter, there is a guy next to me with a sticker over his laptop's camera. Why? Probably because he has read or heard of cases where certain websites or applications gain unauthorized access to your camera and microphone to record you without your knowledge. This invasion of privacy should creep you out a little and cause you to think twice before accepting those extremely long terms and conditions that no one actually reads.

Digital tracking is a popular marketing tool as well. Just recently, my best friend and I were talking on the phone about one of our favorite restaurants. After he hung up, he logged on to Instagram on his phone and an ad appeared in his timeline advertising that very restaurant. It was a tad creepy. Whether or not our phones are actually listening to us all the time, we know that our devices are designed to record massive amounts of data on us each day.

Though Waze gets us to our destinations using the quickest routes, and Netflix finds the perfect shows for us, and Facebook and Google suggest great new products for us to buy based on our viewing habits and places we visit, at what point have we given up too much privacy?

RIGHT TO PRIVACY?

We live in a world of irony. We are willing to post some of the most intimate details and events of our lives online. We gladly sign up for freemium services, like social media and email, that require us to consent to various forms of data tracking in exchange for a free premium service. We love how our devices just know us, as AI empowers them to learn our habits and predict what we will want to see, taste, and even read.

Yet we also feel uneasy and uncomfortable about this. We know that data can be harnessed maliciously. Even as we share everything about ourselves online to garner more likes, shares, and followers, many claim a right to privacy and even support laws and regulations that protect us and our data. The irony is rich, but honestly, we are okay with it for the most part because of the benefits that the tradeoffs afford us each day.

But how are we to navigate these questions about the right to privacy, and how much is too much to share online? How do we know when to stop using certain services or when it is okay to sign up for another? These questions aren't easy and aren't explicitly addressed in Scripture. The Bible doesn't really address the idea of digital privacy head on.

But we can make some judgments based on the overall themes found in the Scriptures and apply those to our questions. We must remember that the Bible doesn't have to address an issue specifically for us to seek wisdom, because if that were the case, we would have no direction on artificial intelligence or even how to use our iPhones. We must see the Bible not as our answer book but as a guide that helps inform us of the best way to live in accordance with God's design and in his grace. So let's start with some foundational truths in our pursuit of privacy in the age of AI.

Complete Privacy Is a Lie

Our God is sovereign over all of creation. Nothing escapes his reach or evades his watchful eye. He knows the number of hairs on our heads (Matt. 10:30) and our passing thoughts. When the Bible talks about God being omniscient or all knowing (Ps. 147:5; Isa. 40:13–14; 44:7–8), it does so to show a distinction between God and human beings, to show that we as God's image-bearers are not gods. There is only one God, and he is able to know all things, even the things we keep secret.

We cannot hide anything from him, nor should we want

to. As his people who know his grace and love, we can be both fully known and fully loved. To paraphrase Tim Keller in his powerful book *The Meaning of Marriage,* being fully known and not loved is one of the scariest things we can experience, and being fully loved without being fully known is a scam.[7]

This rings especially true in a world obsessed with data and privacy. In many cases, we are known by thousands of companies and marketers, but not loved. There is always a bottom line or a quota to be met. For all of the promises companies make about seeking our good and benefiting our lives, those promises will always come second to profit.

Nothing we have ever thought or done will escape God. But while God knows everything about us, he still loves us. God doesn't seek to know us to meet a bottom line. He seeks to know us because of his great love, shown to us in the person and work of his own Son. We cannot hide anything from him, and that is for our good.

Nothing to Hide

Even though we are not able to hide anything from God, does that mean we should be transparent about every area of our lives? While the Bible doesn't specifically address the concepts of privacy that we have today, it does have two overriding principles that should direct how Christians think about privacy.

The book of Acts provides a look inside of the early church and how Christians lived with one another. Acts 2 speaks of how the church broke bread together, met in homes, sat under the apostles' teaching. It also speaks of how the church "had all things in common" (Acts 2:44). According to New Testament scholar John Polhill, this commonality is thought to be based on the Greek ideal of a community in which everything is held in common and shared equally.[8] Polhill writes that this Greek ideal can be traced back as far as the Pythagorean communities that were based on early ideas of a utopian (perfect) community, rather than the one we experience each day that is ravaged by sin. Even though early Christians did not have perfect community with one another (and neither do we), they nonetheless were united by their common love of Christ and one another that flows from being radically changed by the gospel. They didn't need to hide anything from one another because they knew that their hope was found in Christ alone.

The early church didn't have our modern notions of privacy, but they were not nearly as connected with the wider world as we are. Private things in the early church were often seen as communal because of the nature of the church and how the church was to care for one another. Having "all things in common" meant that nothing was kept away from others and from the use of the entire church. This included material things such as money, homes, and property (Acts 2:45) but also included personal sin (James 5:13–16) and even personal details of one's life (Gal. 6:2; 1 John 1:7). They hid nothing from one another because the church is a family, not a social club where one needs to keep things private to gain status or position.

While this openness is good and right for the church, it didn't extend to the same degree to the wider culture. It is not that Christians should keep things from other people per se, but the reason that the church shares things with one another and has "all things in common" is because, as we have said, the church is a family. Family, as we saw in chapter 4, is designed to be one of the safest places for us as human beings,

THE AGE OF AI

a place where we can be the most vulnerable and open with one another.

But we also know that even our families are ravaged by sin and often our families don't feel as safe as they should. Even though the church is a family where we are to look out for one another as well as caring and bearing one another's burdens, the church often fails one another and is a place where many have been hurt. Trust and unity with one another in our families and churches is not something to be assumed but gained over time as we live with one another and build trust. It is a difficult process, but this journey will be fruitful.

As author and technology consultant Chris Ridgeway says, this shifted view of privacy within the community of the church "could be one of the greatest opportunities for witness of this digital decade."[9] We can model how to live without shame, guilt, and fear (Rom. 8:1) as we also model the radical nature of the gospel of Christ and how it transforms our relationships with one another. But as we seek to live in open community as the New Testament church models for us, we also need to be reminded that we live in a dangerous world. From marketing schemes to authoritarian power grabs, our world is a dangerous place because it is broken by sin. Details of our personal lives will be used in malicious ways by those who seek to manipulate and control us.

Data as Property

One of the most common ways we think about privacy is through the lens of personal property. This concept is behind much of the privacy legislation that has been enacted over the past few years, because it ties your privacy to your property. Just as someone can't just take your possessions or steal from you legally, this logic is extended to our digital possessions or property such that you must give permission or access to others to use this data and others are accountable to how they use it. While Christians will apply these truths in a variety of ways to privacy rights, we must keep certain truths central to our thinking about privacy.

Exodus 20:15 gives us some insight into how we are to think about personal property rights, even in our digital age. The eighth commandment states, "You shall not steal." The Ten Commandments sum up the entire law in the Old Testament, thus we know that these commandments hold a lot of concepts together. The eighth commandment has a lot packed into it that can guide us as we think about issues of privacy.

First, we see that we are to love our neighbors and not take advantage of them, because the context of the commandments and the law is each person's being created in God's image. Everything we have has been given to us by God, thus we are not to take or steal things from other people. By stealing what has been given to another, we do two things: deny the dignity of the victim and also proclaim that we must provide for ourselves outside of God's law in contradiction to Matthew 6:25–34, where Jesus tells us not to be anxious about anything because God knows everything we need and will provide.

Second, we see that there is a sense in which the things we have been given by God are our personal stewardship and property until the time of Christ's return (Matthew 13). We have been given everything in this life, including our very lives, in order to glorify God and love our neighbor (Matt. 22:37–39). This property has been entrusted to us and thus is not fair game for others to take from us or for us to take from those around us. In our digital age, we increasingly have digital possessions, and property rights are naturally extended to those things as well. We own digital rights to access content like movies, TV shows, books, and games as well as digital tools and services. Just because something is digital doesn't mean that it can be taken from us without our permission or manipulated toward selfish gains. With the rise of our ever-expanding digital world and the data collected on us each day, we must think wisely about how we wield digital assets and property in ways that honor God and help us to see the dignity and worth of every human being regardless of their perceived value in our society.

Wisdom in Sharing

It is unwise to share all of the details of our lives with the wider world, especially in the age of AI. Because we know that AI feeds off data, we need to be wise with what we share and how we share it. In the world there are bad actors, false prophets, and dangerous people. The Bible speaks of wolves in sheep's clothing who seek to deceive us (Matt. 7:15), and false prophets will claim to be part of the church but are deceiving the people around them. When Jesus sends his followers out on mission into a world desperately in need of hope, he says, "Behold, I am sending you out as sheep in the midst of wolves, so be wise as serpents and innocent as doves" (Matt. 10:16). We are to be innocent, not hiding sin and shame, but also wise. This wisdom is something we cultivate in our hearts over time.

We have a mandate to be wise in how we go about our lives in a sin-torn world. We should not openly share all things with all people but in wisdom openly share the most precious details of our lives with the church. Nothing in this life is truly hidden because we worship a God who knows all things, but we also are called to live in a radical community with one another. In wisdom, we can be transparent with one another because we know that our lives are defined not by our personal information but by the personal sacrifice of Christ on the cross. He gave everything up for us, even though we betrayed him and rebelled against God. As we model radical transparency with one another, we will be able to fight sin and darkness together in light of the new family that God has created.

ARE YOU THE PRODUCT?

From Twitter and Facebook to our digital assistants and music services, we live in the world of low-cost tools that benefit our lives immensely. I mentioned earlier that a tool I find useful is the predictive text feature in my email account. It tries to complete my thoughts or phrases with often creepily good accuracy. The email service can perform this task for me because the AI behind it has access to my entire email database. While the data is not personalized, the AI is trained on this data and grows smarter with every email I send. But these free or cheap services are indeed too good to be true. They aren't free. We pay for them, just often with our data and attention. In turn, our data is processed and packaged to sell to others who want to know what motivates us or what we are thinking. Each time we share these bits of data with others, we are trading a bit of our privacy for convenience.

Have you stopped to consider what those terms and conditions say? The ones we quickly scroll through? Unless you have a law degree, you likely won't understand them. I often scroll as quickly as possible to the bottom or simply click the "agree" button, wanting to move on with my new device or service. But these terms and conditions often tell us the ways that data is being collected on us. Most people unknowingly agree to these collection methods and data uses without much thought because the details are buried in lengthy agreements.

Our viewing history, likes, clicks, and even the time we spend looking at something is being recorded. On the heels of the Facebook data issues surrounding the 2016 presidential election, a gentleman wrote a Twitter thread explaining that companies like Google have been collecting around five giga-bytes of data per user, using this to curate everything from your search results to the online ads you see.[10] Companies are able to see everything we search for, places we go, and things we buy. Our calendars, photos, and notes all help to build a profile of the type of person we are, and that data can be sold to marketers to make a profit. This feels like just the tip of the iceberg of what we know about how our data is being used.

From the failed #DeleteFacebook movement to lawmakers pushing for new consumer privacy regulations, we have been extremely reactive to privacy issues rather than proactive. Privacy is an issue we can't wait to think about in the age of AI. It's up to all of us to engage these moments with proactive discernment and wisdom today, lest we give ourselves away without really knowing it.

WISDOM CALLS

To everyone we meet in person or online we are to model "love, joy, peace, patience, kindness, goodness, faithfulness, gentleness, self-control" (Gal. 5:22–23). But that doesn't mean that we blindly open the personal and private details of our lives to everyone who asks us to agree to their terms and conditions. At times, we will turn down a service or application because in wisdom we believe that level of openness will put us or others at risk. We are to stand up for the vulnerable, weak, and powerless. In the age of AI, that will increasingly mean that we stand up for a person's right to privacy and guard against data exploitation and bias. Data has the power to build up our lives, but also to destroy them. Our personal data has become so valuable that we need to be on the watch for ways that we are selling ourselves to those who have no interest in building us up or guarding our privacy.

Proverbs 1:20 tells us, "Wisdom cries aloud in the street, in the markets she raises her voice." Believers must wisely consider the implications of data mining and other issues of digital privacy.

Promises and agreements will be broken. No company in the world can completely protect your data. What you do online will find you out, because complete privacy is a total lie. Whether from a data leak or hacking, your information is never truly safe. We should assume everything is public and seek to be above reproach in all things, especially our online behavior.

We should also be mindful of how we might be misusing technology. Often we are more controlled by our technology than we control it. We passively embrace new trends or apps without seeing how they might pull us away from glorifying God to glorifying ourselves. Instead of seeking the good of those around us, we can be tempted to seek our own good and live in an algorithm-built world tailored perfectly

What you do online will find you out, because complete privacy is a total lie.

to us. These technologies are often driven by the data we unknowingly give away.

We are responsible for every thought, deed, and click. Nothing has ever escaped the knowledge—or presence—of God. But in this increasingly connected and data-saturated world, it seems nothing will escape those around us either. We must be good stewards of our digital privacy, not because we have something to hide but because prudence demands caution, given who might have access to our data and how it might be used without our knowledge.

It is good and healthy for us to invite others into our lives for the sake of accountability and community. But is it wise to hand over deeply personal details to companies and marketers interested only in the bottom line? And how might this data be used in the future with ever more powerful AI systems, some of which only seem to exist in our dreams? Even as we look to the future of AI, let us not forget that Christians' view of data and privacy will increasingly be at odds with the world around us. But don't step aside; step in and embrace wisdom.

CHAPTER 8

FUTURE

What's Coming Next?

About the time that I started on the journey of writing this book, I was lying on the floor beside our youngest son looking up at the ceiling in his room. He was no more than a few months old at the time. We were both looking around the room and then would look at one another when I made a silly noise that made him laugh. I realized in that moment that he had no concept of what the future will hold for him, nor did I. I might know who is coming for dinner tonight or what we plan to do the next day, but I don't know where he will go to school, whom he will marry (if he does), whether he will have kids of his own, or even what type of work he will pursue. Does his future job even exist right now? What type of technology will he and his family use each day? What issues might he face that I can't even fathom right now? And at the end of his life, how will he remember his mom and dad?

I was lost in my daydream when another laugh brought me back, and I was comforted by the fact that no matter what might come or how advanced our technological innovations may get, nothing will ever change fundamental aspects of the universe. Elon Musk may dream of upgrading humanity with advanced AI to keep up with the robots. Ray Kurzweil may dream of uploading our minds to machines in an effort to overcome our natural limitations. But without a doubt, our God will still be sitting on the throne, and his people, created in his image, will be gathering to praise him. No amount of technological innovation can change that truth. We need not fear the future because we know the one who created all things.

As we dream of the future and the technological innovations to come, it would be wise for us to think about them through the lens of Scripture. Some things are going to change, but many things about our world won't. God calls us to prepare in season and out of season to give a reason for the hope that is within us. We can engage the world around us as it is, not as we hope it to be. The world desperately needs the life-changing message of the gospel and an understanding of our being created in God's image. As we begin this age of AI, we need to understand what we believe and how others think about our world. The time to engage in conversations about technological innovations is now, while they are taking place, rather than responding to them afterward.

LONGING FOR SOMETHING GREATER

We have always been tempted to put our hope in things other than God. We believe that if we just had more money, a loving family, or the newest technology, we would finally be relieved of our burdens. We hope these things will fill the holes in our hearts and make us complete. Every single person, including you and me, knows that there is something fundamentally lacking in us. We know that we are not really the center of the universe and that we cannot know the future. We know there is something greater than us, and we will do anything to transcend how God has created us.

We do this in a multitude of ways, but none greater than trying to make something that we can bow down to and worship. We seek to make things with our own hands that will save us from this world and ultimately from ourselves. I would venture to say that you don't have an idol in your home, a statue of some deity, but I know that you deal with idolatry every day just like I do. Every day we idolize ourselves, our families, our money, and even our technology. We put our trust in these things hoping that they can save us from the despair that we face each day. Putting our hope in anything other than God is the essence of idolatry. The language of idolatry might seem like a foreign concept to you, but God addresses it throughout the Bible.

Isaiah 44:12–17 captures this longing and the creation of idols perfectly:

> The ironsmith takes a cutting tool and works it over the coals. He fashions it with hammers and works it with his strong arm. He becomes hungry, and his strength fails; he drinks no water and is faint. The carpenter stretches a line; he marks it out with a pencil. He shapes it with planes and marks it with a compass. He shapes it into the figure of a man, with the beauty of a man, to dwell in a house. He cuts down cedars, or he chooses a cypress

tree or an oak and lets it grow strong among the trees of the forest. He plants a cedar and the rain nourishes it. Then it becomes fuel for a man. He takes a part of it and warms himself; he kindles a fire and bakes bread. Also he makes a god and worships it; he makes it an idol and falls down before it. Half of it he burns in the fire. Over the half he eats meat; he roasts it and is satisfied. Also he warms himself and says, "Aha, I am warm, I have seen the fire!" And the rest of it he makes into a god, his idol, and falls down to it and worships it. He prays to it and says, "Deliver me, for you are my god!"

The ironsmith makes something with his own hands and then bows down to worship it. What folly! But we are all guilty of this. In our pride and arrogance, we seek our own glory by creating things and believing they will save us. Remember Exodus 32 and the golden calf story that we discussed in chapter 1. We easily forget that God is the one who has made us and saved us. In turning our backs on the creator God to worship the things we make, we ultimately choose to worship ourselves.

So how does this relate to our discussions on AI? Just like every good gift that God has blessed us with, the temptation is to place in these tools hope that they were never designed to carry. We have seen throughout this book that AI can be harnessed in ways that uphold the dignity of every human being and in turn honor God. But the power of AI can also be exploited by sinful and broken humans longing to be like God in ways that leave a trail of broken lives and destruction. The power of these systems tempts us to believe that it is something greater than ourselves and thus deserves to be worshiped. While you probably won't worship your Netflix queue or smart home device, many researchers and developers treat AI as something to be revered because of how this technology will transform our lives. For the first time in history, our creations can mimic and often exceed our own abilities.

But this temptation with technology is nothing new and long preceded the digital computers that we enjoy today. Well before the computer was created, humans were able to create fantastical machines that commanded the hopes and dreams of a generation.

THE FLUTE PLAYER

In 1737, Jacques de Vaucanson completed a masterful work of engineering that left people in awe. Vaucanson was a French inventor and machinist who created some incredibly realistic looking automata, or early robots. The Flute Player, as it was called, was a life-size figure of a shepherd boy that played the tabor and the pipe. It could play twelve songs with its flexible hand and mechanical lungs. This automaton was able to hold the flute up to its mouth and moved its lips to play notes. Depending on hand positions and how hard it blew, it was able to play beautiful music. The flute player moved so naturally that it often drew a crowd. People had seen machines like this before, but not one that moved so easily and could play so many songs.

Reaction to automata was not all excitement and wonder, though. A church official in France had ordered one of Vaucanson's workshops to be destroyed a decade earlier because this official believed that Vaucanson's work was profane. To many, this type of machine seemed like dark magic, and it was something that most people did not understand in that day. Automata worked by using a set of gears and levers intricately designed to play a beautiful song. Automata might not seem as wondrous and magical as they once did, but in that time, they caused people to dream of the future and what might be created.

Just like the Flute Player in the 1730s, today's break-throughs in artificial intelligence cause many to dream of what the future might hold and even to make bold predictions of what will be possible. But just like past generations, the dreams are not always filled with wonder. Often these glimpses of what might be cause us to shudder. The comforting yet often terrifying fact is that for all of our advances in technology spe-cifically with AI, we are still unable to know what will happen tomorrow, much less in fifty to a hundred years from now.

The story of Jesus offers a greater hope than failed visions of the future, a hope that is built on the unchanging and forever God who knows every detail of our future and has promised that he is working all things together for our good and his glory (Rom. 8:28). With this hope in mind, how should we think about the future of AI and where we are headed as a society?

Before we can talk about the impact of these technologies on society, we must understand the debate around the future of AI.

DEFINING TERMS

As we saw in chapter 1, one of the fathers of artificial intelli-gence is John McCarthy. Part of the proposal for the summer research project read "an attempt will be made to find how to make machines use language, form abstractions and concepts, solve kinds of problems now reserved for humans, and improve themselves." The two-month study revealed that many of the early concepts and hallmarks of AI were achievable but proved hard to pull off. This difficulty led many to rethink how the term artificial intelligence was defined.

Some scholars and computer scientists reserve the term artificial intelligence for a general human-like intelligence, which we do not currently have, and there is no consensus that it is even achievable. Others define AI like we have in this book: AI is simply the ability for a machine to perform a complex goal by applying knowledge to the task at hand.

Narrow AI versus General AI (AGI)

As we saw in chapter 1, narrow AI can be applied only in specific ways. These systems are designed to do a singular task or set of tasks rather than to apply skills in a general sense like a human does. Think of Siri on your iPhone or the iRobot vacuum that cleans your home. Current AI systems are not able to think on their own or function outside of their programming.

But many within the AI community are seeking to build a machine that can do just that. They desire to build a system that is able to think on its own and even set its own goals. They dream of a machine that can function wholly independent of human beings as a conscious being that can outperform humans in general intelligence. Some believe that building an AI system to function like or mimic the human brain is the first step in achieving this goal. The term for a general human-level intelligence is often called artificial general intelligence. This AGI is a level of intelligence that can adapt to any situation or problem. It conceivably could perform any task that a human can.

Unlike narrow AI systems such as Deep Blue, which dethroned Garry Kasparov in chess, and AlphaGo, which defeated Lee Sedol in Go, but could do nothing else, AGI would be able not only to learn to play these games but also to wash the dishes, read to your kids, do your homework, and do anything else you ask it to do, and maybe even some things you didn't. It would be able to learn and apply skills across the board, a real-life Rosie for tomorrow's Jetsons.

AGI is often what people think of when they hear of AI systems. An AGI would radically transform our world. It would drastically improve certain aspects of society but lead to great detriment in others. But truthfully, we don't know what these systems might do because we don't even know how to build one. The only general intelligence the world has ever known is a human being. No other creature or technology has ever risen to that level of intelligence. But what if there was something greater than AGI on the horizon?

Superintelligence

Sci-fi movies like *I, Robot*, *The Matrix*, and countless others have been describing a near future in which the robots take over and humanity seems to end. But then suddenly a single person with the will to survive decides to take back the world and restore humanity to its rightful place. Often what we fear, and what is portrayed in these movies, is a more complex level of intelligence called superintelligence.

The concept of superintelligence is believed to have been first laid out in principle by I. J. Good in 1956. Good served as the statistician on Alan Turing's code-breaking team during World War II. Good wrote, "Let an ultraintelligent machine be defined as a machine that can far surpass all of the intellectual activities of any man however clever. Since the design of machines is one of these intellectual activities, an ultraintelligent machine could design even better machines;

there would then unquestionably be an 'intelligence explosion,' and the intelligence of man would be left far behind. Thus, the first intelligent machine is the last invention that man need ever make, provided that the machine is docile enough to tell us how to keep it under control."[1]

Superintelligence, or, as Good called it, ultraintelligence, is simply a machine that is self-improving and more intelligent than a human being in every conceivable way. But all of this is possible only if we are able to attain AGI. The argument for an AGI follows from the logic that humanity is nothing more than a set of organic algorithms or analog machines.[2] Harari describes humanity as "an obsolete algorithm."[3] This naturalist and materialist worldview is the complete opposite of what Christians believe about ourselves and this world. The argument follows that if we are nothing more than a computer system that can exhibit emotions, thoughts, and opinions, then we should be able to design digital machines that do the same things and someday surpass us. But is there a moment when this breakthrough in AI might take place and our entire world change?

THE SINGULARITY

You may have heard of this coming moment called the singularity. Maybe from your favorite sci-fi film or novel. Or maybe you have heard of Ray Kurzweil and his bold predictions from his famous works *The Age of Spiritual Machines* or *The Singularity Is Near*. Often the singularity is defined as a moment that leads to doomsday, a dystopian future where humanity loses control of AI and robots. In these descriptions of the future, humans are at worst killed off or at best become zoo animals to be enjoyed by superintelligent robots, which represent the next phase of evolutionary life on this planet (and probably others).[4]

The term singularity is said to have been first used in the 1950s by John von Neumann, a Hungarian-American mathematician, physicist, and computer scientist. His colleague and friend Ulam Stanislaw wrote about a conversation with Von Neumann that "centered on the accelerating progress of technology and changes in the mode of human life, which gives the appearance of approaching some essential singularity in the history of the race beyond which human affairs, as we know them, could not continue."[5]

This singularity is simply an event horizon or the moment when computer intelligence, AGI, exceeds human-level intelligence. We can't see past this horizon because of the limitations of the human mind. At the singularity, human history would be changed forever and machines would become so advanced that they would take over our world and continue to improve themselves through reprogramming.

The argument for the singularity rests on two main pillars: exponentially improving computer systems and the understanding that humanity is nothing more than a machine. As computers have grown faster and cheaper each year since their invention, Moore's Law has been the prevailing understanding of the exponential growth of computing power. It is named after Gordon Moore, who cofounded Intel. Moore's Law states that the number of transistors in computers' integrated circuits doubles every two years. The greater the number of transistors, the higher the processing power in computer systems, which drives the complexity of AI systems.

This exponential growth of computing power has been true

since 1950. At the publication of this book, it still holds true, though some have argued that it will soon no longer hold because it won't be possible to make transistors any smaller. New theories of chip design include quantum computing are becoming popular with companies like Google and Microsoft pursuing this revolutionary technology. Originally, computers were the size of a small house, and now you wear one on your wrist that is much more powerful than it was imagined they'd ever be even twenty years ago. Technology has experienced this exponential growth in large part because of Moore's Law and human ingenuity.

The argument for AGI and for the singularity states that if we have adequate computing power, then the only thing lacking is the ability to copy or mimic the human mind. If human beings are nothing more than machines, then computers can supplant us because they not only will mimic us but outperform us in every aspect of life. They would be able to attain consciousness and supplant humanity as the most advanced life form in the universe.

The popularity of the materialistic understanding of humanity in our society is one of the main reasons that the singularity has gained so much notoriety in the last few years. The thinking is that we have computers that can become masters at chess, Go, and even StarCraft, so we must be near the singularity where an intelligent machine supplants us as the highest order of creation.

As Jaan Tallinn, codeveloper of Skype, says, in reference to the coming singularity and rise of superintelligence, "Look around you—you're witnessing the final decades of a hundred-thousand-year regime."[6] In response to Tallinn, we simply have to say that if you get the starting point of humanity wrong, it seems that you also getting the ending wrong.

If all of this sounds more like a sci-fi movie plot to you, you are not alone. This is a hotly debated topic within some areas of artificial intelligence and one that has no foreseeable conclusion. We simply do not know whether human-level AI is even possible, much less when this moment of singularity might occur. But we do know that to attain that level of sophistication with artificial intelligence, we must first develop a computer with a consciousness, or at least one that would be considered general AI.

CONSCIOUS COMPUTERS?

One day in the future, will our computers just wake up and decide to take over the world? Will they try to enslave us? I don't think so. Even if our machines ever obtain a general level of intelligence, the progression from narrow to general will be much more gradual than many think. We won't wake up one day to find our smart devices taking over our houses, or our cars suddenly deciding to take us to the woods to leave us for dead. The development of general AI will be slow, taking place in incremental steps, and likely we will see it coming. But that doesn't mean that we shouldn't think through how to develop such AI with safety and human dignity in mind.

But what is consciousness, anyway? Simply put, consciousness is the ability to know that you exist. It is being aware, having the ability to think about thinking.

Current AI systems do not have anything close to consciousness. They simply follow commands and protocols designed by human beings. These tools perform the tasks and goals that we set for them, and do not have the ability or the will to change those goals. They are not aware that they exist and do not understand many of the answers they give us. They simply perform the action and it is up to us to interpret the results. While they may perform tasks in ways that surprise us, they are not conscious of doing it. They simply perform the goal in a way that is more efficient than their human programmers think is possible.

We know, though, that consciousness or self-awareness doesn't determine value or worth. We see various levels of consciousness throughout the animal kingdom. Our family's miniature schnauzer is conscious of his own existence, exhibiting self-awareness, emotions, and a desire to protect himself, but not on the level even of my toddler. And my dog and my son are orders of magnitude different in value and dignity. While it is cruel and wrong to hurt an animal, most people would not equate abuse of an animal with that of a person. Both abuses are wrong, but on different levels. The reason that my son is more valuable than my dog is based solely on the fact that God created humanity in his image and made dogs lower than humanity in creation.

If consciousness is our main reason for creating superintelligent machines, then many people are going to be sorely disappointed. I believe that we will continue to achieve great feats of computer programming and development of artificial intelligence. I believe that humanity has not reached its peak in our ability to create new technologies. As Sean Gerrish says, "These [future] machines will follow programs that will grow more and more complex, and it will become more and more difficult to discern what they're doing, but it will always be possible to trace every action they perform back to a deterministic set of instructions."[7] While Gerrish states that humans are just analog machines, he highlights here a difference between man and machine that is profound.

Humanity cannot be defined as a computer program the

way that an AI system can. God did not program us or design us to carry out a set of instructions. We were created by God and given free will, and yet God still knows all things that will take place on heaven and earth. God is not like humans and doesn't think about the world like we do. He is orders of magnitude higher in value than humanity, and humanity is likewise orders of magnitude higher in value than even the most advanced machine that will ever be created.

UTOPIAN DREAMS

Rather than belabor the point about whether it is possible to develop general AI or superintelligence, we should look at when some people predict such developments might occur and see what is behind their dreams. A 2016 survey of AI researchers shows that the idea of human-level AI is growing in popularity. More than 50 percent of those surveyed believe that by 2040 to 2050 we will have AGI, and 75 percent believe that thirty years after obtaining AGI, we will have superintelligent machines.[8]

Bill Joy, cofounder of Sun Microsystems, warns of self-replicating robots and advances in biotechnology that could result in AI taking over the human species as early as 2030,[9] while Hans Moravec of the AI lab at Carnegie Mellon claims that by 2040 "we will finally achieve the original goal of robotics and a thematic mainstay of science fiction: a freely moving machine with the intellectual capabilities of a human being."[10] Moravec suggests a similar timeline to the moment of singularity as Ray Kurzweil, who predicts the date as 2045, with 2029 being the year that we achieve some level of general intelligence.

As Kai-Fu Lee describes in his book *AI Superpowers,* many of these folks "see the dawn of AGI and the subsequent singularity as the final frontier in human flourishing, an opportunity to expand our own consciousness and conquer mortality."[11] This is what drives the conversation about the possibility of human-level intelligence. Deep down each of us knows that this world is broken and that we are not adequate to fix it on our own. For most people in our society, the longing for something greater than ourselves to solve our world's problems and injustices is tied to some level of intelligence outside of ourselves, like AGI. We are, indeed, looking for a savior.

We are, indeed, looking for a savior.

FINAL THOUGHTS

While I applaud the growing consensus that we must develop ethical AI and invest in AI safety research, I believe that we must go farther than creating safe AI. To me, the greatest danger is not humanity designing an AI system that will take over the world but humanity using AI tools in ways that dishonor God and our fellow image-bearers. Christians must be the ones who champion the dignity of every human life, not just the ones in the womb or on their deathbeds. We must also champion the ones who are increasingly seen by our society as disposable because they might not have the right stuff to contribute to society. When we value someone based on their utility, we rob them of their God-given dignity and rights. These are not ours to assign or remove. Only God has that ability, and what he said about us will never change. The things of this earth will pass away, but he will remain.

The psalmist tells us in Psalm 102:25–27:

> Of old you laid the foundation of the earth,
>   and the heavens are the work of your hands.
> They will perish, but you will remain;
>   they will all wear out like a garment.
> You will change them like a robe, and they will pass away,
>   but you are the same, and your years have no end.

I don't fear AI or even the moment of singularity. I don't fear robots, even if one day they do wake up with some level of consciousness. Rather, I fear the people of God buying the lie that we are nothing more than machines and that somehow AI will usher in a utopian age. AI is not a savior. It is not going to fix all of our world's problems. It is a tool that must be wielded with wisdom. AI will lead to many great advances but also will open up new opportunities to dishonor God and devalue our neighbor. Just as technology always has.

God-given dignity isn't ours to assign or remove.

Onward to the future, full of joy, expectation, and hope as we seek to navigate the age of AI as the people of God.

ACKNOWLEDGMENTS

This project has been a labor of love, and I would never have been able to cross the finish line without the help and support of so many.

While words are not adequate for the way she has loved me, I want to thank my wife, who has sacrificed so much so that I could pursue this project. Without her love and support, it would not have been possible. She is the love of my life, and I can't express how thankful I am for her and our family. To my boys: I love each of you more than you know.

I want to thank my mentor and colleague, Dan Darling, who has been one of the strongest and most encouraging advocates of this project. He was the first to encourage me to pursue writing and provided me with invaluable advice and support along the way. I also want to thank Josh Wester, Alex Ward, and Seth Woodley, each of whom has listened to me process this project out loud, as well as read and edited countless drafts. My communications colleagues, Lindsay Nicolet and

Marie Delph, have also read countless articles over the years as this project developed. Many people have read the manuscript and given incredibly helpful feedback along the way, including Brian Dellinger and Michael Hilton. I also want to thank Brent Leatherwood and Andrew Walker for their encouragement and feedback over these past few years.

I am incredibly thankful for the leadership of the Ethics and Religious Liberty Commission, including Russell Moore and Phillip Bethancourt, who have allowed me space and encouraged me to pursue this work. I cannot express my gratitude enough to the entire team at Zondervan, including my editors Andy Rogers and Brian Phipps, who believed in this project and spent countless hours helping to craft and polish this work. And extra thanks to my agent, Erik Wolgemuth, and his team for their support and dedication to this work.

Finally, to my mom and dad: for everything that you have done for me and for the constant love and support you have shown me throughout my life, I thank God for each of you.

NOTES

Chapter 1: Foundation

1. Ray Kurzweil, *How to Create a Mind: The Secret of Human Thought Revealed* (New York: Viking, 2012), 158.
2. "Gutenberg's Legacy and Populism," *Axios,* https://www.axios.com/gutenberg-legacy-political-social-turmoil-bb4f930c-2cb4-4ddc-99be-2ff9464b0827.html.
3. It should be noted that it is still unknown how much was programmed and how much was learned by the robots from Boston Dynamics, which has kept many details of their creations under wraps.
4. "A Proposal for the Dartmouth Summer Research Project on Artificial Intelligence," Stanford University, November 24, 2019, http://jmc.stanford.edu/articles/dartmouth.html.
5. Karen Gilchrist, "Alibaba Launches 'Smile to Pay' Facial Recognition System at KFC in China," *CNBC,* September 4, 2017, https://www.cnbc.com/2017/09/04/alibaba-launches-smile-to-pay-facial-recognition-system-at-kfc-china.html.
6. Max Tegmark, *Life 3.0: Being Human in the Age of Artificial Intelligence* (New York: Knopf, 2017), 29.
7. Yuval Noah Harari, *Homo Deus: A Brief History of Tomorrow,* Vintage Popular Science (London: Harvill Secker, 2016), 323.

Chapter 2: Self

1. James L. Olds and Lily Whiteman, "Exploring the Unknown Frontier of the Brain," National Science Foundation, April 2, 2015, https://www.nsf.gov/discoveries/disc_summ.jsp?cntn_id=134653.
2. Jay W. Richards, *The Human Advantage: The Future of American Work in an Age of Smart Machines* (New York: Crown Forum, 2018), 198.
3. G. K. Beale, *We Become What We Worship: A Biblical Theology of Idolatry* (Downers Grove, Ill.: InterVarsity, 2008), 16.
4. Benjamin E. Sasse, *Them: Why We Hate Each Other and How to Heal* (New York: St. Martin's Press, 2018), 4.
5. Richards, *The Human Advantage,* 197.
6. Emily Esfahani Smith, *The Power of Meaning: Crafting a Life That Matters* (New York: Crown, 2017), 55.
7. Yuval Noah Harari, *Homo Deus: A Brief History of Tomorrow,* Vintage Popular Science (London: Harvill Secker, 2016), 341.
8. "The Smart Audio Report," accessed November 24, 2019, https://www.nationalpublicmedia.com/smart-audio-report/latest-report/.
9. Ronan De Renesse, "Virtual Digital Assistants to Overtake World Population by 2021," Ovum, May 17, 2017, https://ovum.informa.com/resources/product-content/virtual-digital-assistants-to-overtake-world-population-by-2021.
10. Judith Shulevitz, "Alexa, Should We Trust You?" *The Atlantic,* November 2018, https://www.theatlantic.com/magazine/archive/2018/11/alexa-how-will-you-change-us/570844/.
11. Ibid.

Chapter 3: Medicine

1. "Limb Loss Statistics," *Amputee Coalition* (blog), accessed December 7, 2018, https://www.amputee-coalition.org/resources/limb-loss-statistics/.
2. Yuval Noah Harari, *Homo Deus: A Brief History of Tomorrow,* Vintage Popular Science (London: Harvill Secker, 2016), 2.
3. Ibid., 21.
4. "Doctors Said the Coma Patients Would Never Wake. AI Said They Would—and They Did," *South China Morning Post,* September 8, 2018, https://www.scmp.com/news/china/science/

article/2163298/doctors-said-coma-patients-would-never-wake
-ai-said-they-would.

5. Harari, *Homo Deus*, 318.

6. Eric J. Topol, *Deep Medicine: How Artificial Intelligence Can Make Healthcare Human Again* (New York: Basic Books, 2019), 21.

7. Chi Wan Koo et al., "Improved Efficiency of CT Interpretation Using an Automated Lung Nodule Matching Program," *American Journal of Roentgenology* 199, no. 1 (July 2012): 91–95, https://doi.org/10.2214/AJR.11.7522.

8. Kai-Fu Lee, *AI Superpowers: China, Silicon Valley, and the New World Order* (Boston: Houghton Mifflin Harcourt, 2018), 155.

9. Samuel R. Schroerlucke et al., "Complication Rate in Robotic-Guided vs Fluoro-Guided Minimally Invasive Spinal Fusion Surgery: Report from MIS Refresh Prospective Comparative Study," *The Spine Journal* 17, no. 10 (October 1, 2017): S254–55, https://doi.org/10.1016/j.spinee.2017.08.177.

10. "Family Credits Apple Watch for Saving Daughter's Life," ABC News, May 2, 2018, https://goodmorningamerica.com /wellness/story/family-credits-apple-watch-saving-daughters -life-54853328.

11. Richard Godwin, "'We Will Get Regular Body Upgrades': What Will Humans Look Like in 100 Years?" *The Guardian*, September 22, 2018, sec. Life and Style, https://www.the guardian.com/lifeandstyle/2018/sep/22/regular-body-upgrades -what-will-humans-look-like-in-100-years.

12. Andrea Powell, "AI Is Fueling Smarter Prosthetics Than Ever Before," *Wired*, December 22, 2017, https://www.wired.com /story/ai-is-fueling-smarter-prosthetics-than-ever-before/.

13. Peter Biello, "N.H. Vet Becomes First Fitted with Two 'LUKE' Arms," accessed June 12, 2019, https://www.nhpr.org/post/nh -vet-becomes-first-fitted-two-luke-arms.

Chapter 4: Family

1. See susancbennett.com. Bennett didn't know her voice would end up as a voice assistant when she recorded the audio in 2005.

2. "New Voicebot Report Says Nearly 20% of U.S. Adults Have Smart Speakers," Voicebot, March 7, 2018, https://voicebot.ai

/2018/03/07/new-voicebot-report-says-nearly-20-u-s-adults
-smart-speakers/.

3. Stefania Druga, "Growing Up with AI: How Can Families Play
   and Learn with Their New Smart Toys and Companions?"
   MIT Media Lab, accessed December 19, 2018, https://www
   .media.mit.edu/posts/growing-up-with-ai-how-can-families
   -play-and-learn-with-their-new-smart-toys-and-companions/.

4. Alexis C. Madrigal, "Should Children Form Emotional Bonds with
   Robots?" *The Atlantic,* November 7, 2017, https://www.theatlantic
   .com/magazine/archive/2017/12/my-sons-first-robot/544137/.

5. Russell Moore, *The Storm-Tossed Family: How the Cross Reshapes
   the Home* (Nashville: B&H Publishing Group, 2018), 229.

6. Judith Shulevitz, "Alexa, Should We Trust You?" *The Atlantic,*
   November 2018, https://www.theatlantic.com/magazine
   /archive/2018/11/alexa-how-will-you-change-us/570844/.

7. Tara Isabella Burton, "We're Talking about 'Sex Robots' Now.
   We've Been Here Before," *Vox,* May 4, 2018, https://www.vox
   .com/2018/5/4/17314260/incel-sex-robots-sexual-redistribution
   -ross-douthat-history.

8. Chaim Gartenberg, "Mark Zuckerberg: 'We Want to Get a
   Billion People in Virtual Reality,'" *The Verge*, October 11, 2017,
   https://www.theverge.com/2017/10/11/16459636/mark-zucker
   berg-oculus-rift-connect.

9. Benjamin E. Sasse, *The Vanishing American Adult: Our
   Coming-of-Age Crisis—and How to Rebuild a Culture of Self-
   Reliance* (New York: St. Martin's Press, 2017), 242.

Chapter 5: Work

1. Harvard Health Publishing, "Moderate Exercise: No Pain,
   Big Gains," *Harvard Health,* accessed October 21, 2018,
   https://www.health.harvard.edu/newsletter_article/Moderate
   _exercise_No_pain_big_gains.

2. Timothy Keller and Katherine Leary Alsdorf, *Every Good
   Endeavor: Connecting Your Work to God's Work* (New York:
   Dutton, 2012), 49.

3. Jay W. Richards, *The Human Advantage: The Future of
   American Work in an Age of Smart Machines* (New York:
   Crown Forum, 2018), 18.

4. Walter Russell Mead, "Beyond Blue Part One: The Crisis of the American Dream," *The American Interest* (blog), January 29, 2012, https://www.the-american-interest.com/2012/01/29/beyond-blue-part-one-the-crisis-of-the-american-dream/.

5. G. K. Kasparov and Mig Greengard, *Deep Thinking: Where Machine Intelligence Ends and Human Creativity Begins* (New York: PublicAffairs, 2017), 19–20.

6. Alex Rosenblat, *Uberland: How Algorithms Are Rewriting the Rules of Work* (Oakland, Calif.: University of California Press, 2018), 98.

7. Ibid., 148–49.

8. Yuval N. Harari, *21 Lessons for the 21st Century* (New York: Spiegel and Grau, 2018), 20.

9. Max Tegmark, *Life 3.0: Being Human in the Age of Artificial Intelligence* (New York: Knopf, 2017), 121–22.

10. Richards, *The Human Advantage*, 184.

Chapter 6: War

1. Paul Scharre, *Army of None: Autonomous Weapons and the Future of War* (New York: Norton, 2018), 36.

2. "Summa Theologiae: War (Secunda Secundae Partis, Q. 40)," accessed June 4, 2019, http://www.newadvent.org/summa/3040.htm.

3. Scharre, *Army of None,* 39.

4. Ibid., 44.

5. "Samsung Reveals SGR-1 Robot Sentry Set to Keep an Eye on North Korea," *Daily Mail Online,* accessed March 8, 2019, https://www.dailymail.co.uk/sciencetech/article-2756847/Who-goes-Samsung-reveals-robot-sentry-set-eye-North-Korea.html.

6. Scharre, *Army of None*, 318.

7. "Israel Aerospace Industries Unveils 'Mini Harpy,' Its New Loitering Munition," Intelligent Aerospace, accessed June 4, 2019, https://www.intelligent-aerospace.com/military/article/16543585/israel-aerospace-industries-unveils-mini-harpy-its-new-loitering-munition.

8. "Pentagon: 'No One Will Ever Know' How Many Civilians US Has Killed in Fight against ISIS," *Stars and Stripes,* accessed March 8, 2019, https://www.stripes.com/news/middle-east/

pentagon-no-one-will-ever-know-how-many-civilians-us-has
-killed-in-fight-against-isis-1.531275.

9. Daniel L. Byman, "Why Drones Work: The Case for Washington's
Weapon of Choice," *Brookings* (blog), November 30, 2001, https://
www.brookings.edu/articles/why-drones-work-the-case-for
-washingtons-weapon-of-choice/.

10. See US Department of Defense directive 3000.09 at https://
www.esd.whs.mil/Portals/54/Documents/DD/issuances/dodd
/300009p.pdf?ver=2019-02-25-104306-377.

11. "'The Business of War': Google Employees Protest Work for the
Pentagon," *New York Times,* accessed March 11, 2019, https://
www.nytimes.com/2018/04/04/technology/google-letter-ceo
-pentagon-project.html.

12. "Amazon's Jeff Bezos Says Tech Companies Should Work with
the Pentagon," *Wired,* accessed March 11, 2019, https://www
.wired.com/story/amazons-jeff-bezos-says-tech-companies
-should-work-with-the-pentagon/.

13. "Autonomous Weapons: An Open Letter from AI and Robotics
Researchers," Future of Life Institute, accessed March 27,
2019, https://futureoflife.org/open-letter-autonomous-weapons/.

14. "1960 Presidential Visit to Seattle by U.S. Senator John F.
Kennedy," JackGordon.org, accessed June 4, 2019, http://
jackgordon.org/Events/1960-jfk-senator.htm.

Chapter 7: Data and Privacy

1. Seth Stephens-Davidowitz and Steven Pinker, *Everybody Lies:
Big Data, New Data, and What the Internet Can Tell Us about
Who We Really Are* (New York: Dey St., 2017), 21.

2. To read the entire story of the exodus, see Genesis 37 through
Exodus 14.

3. "This Clever AI Hid Data from Its Creators to Cheat at Its
Appointed Task," *TechCrunch* (blog), accessed February 11,
2019, http://social.techcrunch.com/2018/12/31/this-clever-ai
-hid-data-from-its-creators-to-cheat-at-its-appointed-task/.

4. "How Will Artificial Intelligence Shape Mortgage Lending?"
accessed February 11, 2019, http://www.fanniemae.com
/resources/file/research/mlss/pdf/mlss-artificial-intelligence
-100418.pdf.

5. Shai Danziger, Jonathan Levav, and Liora Avnaim-Pesso, "Extraneous Factors in Judicial Decisions," *Proceedings of the National Academy of Sciences* 108, no. 17 (April 26, 2011): 6889–92, https://doi.org/10.1073/pnas.1018033108.

6. Prison Policy Initiative and Peter Wagner and Wendy Sawyer, "Mass Incarceration: The Whole Pie 2018," accessed February 15, 2019, https://www.prisonpolicy.org/reports/pie2018.html.

7. Timothy Keller and Kathy Keller, *The Meaning of Marriage: Facing the Complexities of Commitment with the Wisdom of God* (New York: Dutton, 2011), 95.

8. John B. Polhill, *Acts,* The New American Commentary, vol. 26 (Nashville: Broadman Press, 1992).

9. Chris Ridgeway, "Fixing Our Privacy Settings," Christianity Today.com, accessed June 8, 2019, https://www.christianity today.com/ct/2018/september/theology-of-privacy-fixing-our -settings.html.

10. "Dylan Curran on Twitter: 'Want to Freak Yourself Out? I'm Gonna Show Just How Much of Your Information the Likes of Facebook and Google Store about You without You Even Realising It,'" Twitter, accessed June 7, 2019, https://twitter .com/iamdylancurran/status/977559925680467968.

Chapter 8: Future

1. Irving John Good, "Speculations concerning the First Ultraintelligent Machine," in *Advances in Computers*, ed. Franz L. Alt and Morris Rubinoff, vol. 6 (Amsterdam: Elsevier, 1966), 31–88, https://doi.org/10.1016/S0065-2458(08)60418-0.

2. Sean Gerrish, *How Smart Machines Think* (Cambridge, Mass.: MIT Press, 2018), 266.

3. Yuval Noah Harari, *Homo Deus: A Brief History of Tomorrow,* Vintage Popular Science (London: Harvill Secker, 2016), 348.

4. Max Tegmark, *Life 3.0: Being Human in the Age of Artificial Intelligence* (New York: Knopf, 2017), 162–63.

5. Ulam Stanislaw, "Tribute to John von Neumann," *Bulletin of the American Mathematical Society* 64, no. 3 (May 1958): 49.

6. John Brockman, ed., *Possible Minds: Twenty-Five Ways of Looking at AI* (New York: Penguin, 2019), 94.

7. Gerrish, *How Smart Machines Think,* 266.

8. Vincent C. Müller and Nick Bostrom, "Future Progress in Artificial Intelligence: A Survey of Expert Opinion," in *Fundamental Issues of Artificial Intelligence*, ed. Vincent C. Müller (Cham: Springer International Publishing, 2016), 555–72, https://doi.org/10.1007/978-3-319-26485-1_33.

9. "Why the Future Doesn't Need Us," *Wired,* accessed February 22, 2019, https://www.wired.com/2000/04/joy-2/.

10. Hans Moravec, "Rise of the Robots: The Future of Artificial Intelligence," *Scientific American,* accessed February 22, 2019, https://www.scientificamerican.com/article/rise-of-the-robots/.

11. Kai-Fu Lee, *AI Superpowers: China, Silicon Valley, and the New World Order* (Boston: Houghton Mifflin Harcourt, 2018), 140.